D1381324

HOW TO BE A GURU

BOOKS BY GEORGE MIKES

GEORGE MIKES

How to be a Guru

Illustrated by
LARRY

ANDRE DEUTSCH

First published in 1984 by
André Deutsch Limited
105 Great Russell Street London WC1

Photoptypeset by
Wyvern Typesetting Limited, Bristol
Printed in Great Britain by
Ebenezer Baylis and Son Ltd
Worcester

ISBN 0 233 97707 4

To Alex and Harry,
to remind them of their wise old grandfather

Contents

The Sugared Pill

The Sugared Pill

I AM A VERY wise man. Not terribly intelligent, highly educated or brilliantly clever, but very wise.

About a quarter of a century ago, I wrote a little book entitled *Wisdom for Others*. The title referred to a maxim of La Rochefoucauld: "It is easier to be wise for others than for yourself." This is as true now as it was at the beginning of the fifties, or indeed in the seventeenth century when La Rochefoucauld penned the remark, soon after the end of the Thirty Years War. And it was true, too, a few years after the end of the Peloponnesian War and a few thousand years before *that*. Since I am about to be wise for others for the second time, the permanence of this truth is welcome.

This book contains the collected wisdom of a lifetime. Consequently it is a serious book, like all my other books. A few people will nod in approval. Many others will frown: if it is a serious book of true wisdom why the funny drawings? Why the jokes and anecdotes which will – well, may – make people laugh? Indeed, why the very title: *How to be a Guru*? A real Guru is an oriental sage (at least that is what he alleges, and his disciples believe it) and while I may be as wise as any one of them, I certainly am no Bengali or Tamil. The word *guru*, when applied to a European, has an ironic or even derogatory (in this case self-derogatory) ring. Why this self-mockery when I wish to be taken seriously?

There are a number of answers to these questions. One is that I *am* serious but do not necessarily want to be taken seriously. Another is that this form of expression is prompted by cowardice. As I shall explain later, cowardice is one of the dominant forces and motives of human development and, on the whole, it is a beneficial and commendable influence. Cowardice is the foundation stone of *all* religions; it is also the foundation stone of humour. The humorist – and even the clown is no exception – is desirous, occasionally desperate, to say something serious but does not dare to. *He is afraid of being laughed at.* To be afraid of being laughed at is the basic trauma of the humorist. So he wraps up his message to the world in jokes. There is an apologetic smile on his lips: it is all a joke, please note that even I am not taking myself seriously. The threat of *not* being laughed at when joking is not half as tormenting as the threat of being laughed at when talking seriously.

The cowardice of the humorist provokes a well-deserved but nevertheless false reaction from the public and the literary pundits. When he insists "Look, I am only being funny," they believe him. Being believed can cause immense tragedies (think of mediaeval priests preaching hell-fire), but I am not talking of immense tragedies at the moment, just of vexations, irritations, misunderstandings. People are inclined to believe that something uttered with a serious face and a throbbing voice is indeed serious while something (perhaps the same thing) expressed in a jocular manner and garnished with anecdotes, must be altogether a joke and should be dismissed with a knowing smile. But the form of expression has no more to do with the validity of the idea than the colour of food has with its taste or nutritional value. I have never heard the remark: "Red food – beef, beetroot, red wine – is good; green food – lettuce, spinach, white wine – is bad" (or vice versa). To judge a piece of writing by the same principle – by its colour, so to say – is not more intelligent. To hold that something expressed with pomposity, in complicated sentences full of Graeco-Roman jargon *must* be profound

2

(sometimes it is), while something expressed in a light-hearted, readable and entertaining manner *must* be superficial and trivial (it can be) is no better than loving beetroot because it is red and rejecting lettuce because it is green.

Or put it in another way. Medicine must often be bitter. But the pill may be sweetened, and it is possible for a sugared pill to be just as curative as a bitter and revolting one. And it is pleasanter to swallow.

Part One: General Wisdom

The Beholder's Eye

THE MATTER, HOWEVER, is not quite as simple as that. It is not up to you whether you express yourself lightheartedly or gloomily, enjoyably or clumsily; whether you see life as an endless bonanza or a chain of unmitigated disasters; whether you take blows with a shrug of the shoulder or with suicidal despair; whether you expect everything to turn out well or are always full of anxiety, foreboding and dejection.

You do not *choose* your temperament. You do not choose your philosophy either. A philosophy chooses you. You think that some statement of opinion suddenly fills your mind with light, but in fact, the opinion was yours already, even though you may not have been aware of it. You do not become a fascist or a neo-nazi because a rousing speech at a National Front meeting has convinced you. You would not have gone to that meeting if you had not had the seed of agreement in you.

Sometimes the so-called philosophy is of secondary importance. You may join a movement (fascists, trotskyites, punk rockers, anything) because you are terrified of loneliness and need to belong to some group which gives you warmth and a feeling of superiority. This is your real aim and it does not matter much – it may be the result of pure chance – which group you join.

Or imagine a young man, burning with overpowering ambition. He wants fame, power and glory and decides that politics are the way to achieve them. Very well, but which party to join? He sits down and ponders. He is a well-educated man of aristocratic background so the Tory Party would be his natural and obvious choice – but the Tory Party is full of young hopefuls like himself. It is the Labour Party that really needs well-educated, well-spoken public-school boys. There he has rarity value. At the same time he will be suspect: what is a young aristocrat with an Oxbridge degree and accent doing in the Labour ranks? Very fishy. So he has to prove himself. He has to express his unshakeable Socialism louder and louder, and will be pushed – will push himself – farther and farther to the left. He may find himself the leader of the left. After a while he will most sincerely believe in his Socialist principles because he has invested a whole life in them, his success is built on them, and if he did not believe in them with the utmost sincerity he would have to despise himself: sincere conviction has become a necessary self-defence. Yet it was the toss of a coin which made him a Socialist. The idea for which he is ready to sacrifice his life – for which he is actually sacrificing his life – is far more deeply rooted: it is not the victory of Socialism but the glory of himself.

If I am right – as I am – in saying that you cannot choose your philosophy but your philosophy chooses you, then the obvious question arises: what is the point in writing this book? If one cannot convince anyone, why try? If no one can be persuaded, why not save the effort?

The effort remains worthwhile. The less important reason for going on writing is that while philosophy is unlikely to convert it may still enlighten, entertain and provoke thought. Whatever any philosopher has said in the past has always been contradicted at once by other philosophers who not only tried to refute his theses, but also called him an ass (usually, but not always, in polite language). A great many brilliant and inspiring things have been said which remained brilliant and inspiring

8

regardless of whether they were right or wrong. Throughout the history of philosophy, *what* was said has always been less important than *how* it was said. Dazzling arguments leading to false conclusions have always carried more weight and been more celebrated than sound thinking served up in a sauce of dullness.

But there is a more important reason for persevering. You cannot convince, still less convert, anyone – that is true. People will always choose the philosophy the seeds of which they have been carrying in their souls or brains. But perhaps *mine* is the philosophy the seeds of which you are carrying? You will have to read what I am going to say before you can tell. Although no one can really convert anybody, it is possible to bring out what other people contain: treasures which might otherwise remain buried forever.

If my philosophy suits you, you will not become a more brilliant and intellectual person than you were before, but you will be happier, better pleased with your lot. I am not Aristotle or Descartes. But it is better to mine iron ore than to leave it undiscovered in the stomach of the earth just because you can't get at true gold.

So no one is in a position to decide whether he will be a fascist or a moderate, an optimist or a pessimist, indolent or anxious, funny or gloomy. Neither can he decide the style in which he will write. In my early days in England Ivor Novello put on a low-brow musical, *There Shall Be No Night*, which was a colossal success. At the same time T. S. Eliot's new play was a bit of a commercial flop. Eliot could not say, even if he had been so inclined: "To hell with it! I'll now write a low-brow musical, just to make a lot of money." He could no more do that than Ivor Novello could write *The Waste Land*. To climb Everest is a great feat, to descend it is no easier.

9

I cannot help being what I am. And this is my second reason for writing the way I do – the first one being my cowardice.

Humour is in the beholder's eye. As a matter of fact, pretty well everything is in the beholder's eye. Happiness – this most discussed dream of humanity – has very little to do with fate (except in extreme and rare circumstances). It has everything to do with your ability to be contented. The story of the poor little rich girl may be rubbish from the literary point of view but it is one of the basic moral tales of human destiny. Poor girls can easily be happier than rich girls. But rich girls may be happy too. Climb high, by all means. There is nothing wrong with ambition, which is there to be fulfilled. But having climbed, then enjoy the height. Do not get dizzy and do not worry about the few who have climed higher still.

Second thought. For a long time I, as a beholder, was convinced that humour – as I have just pronounced – was in my eyes. I could not help seeing everything around me as grotesque, funny, contradictory. That was how and why I had been labelled as a humorist. I could not help it, that was my destiny, the inevitable result of my genes and my early upbringing. Through no fault of my own I reflected a distorted image of the world.

Then slowly, very slowly, it dawned on me that I was mistaken. *I see the world as it is*. It is the world that is grotesque, funny, and paradoxical, not my view of it. It is the world that is distorted, not my vision. I am a sober observer, objective and matter-of-fact. It is the world that is crazy.

The Other Way Round

LET'S START, THEN, with some simple examples of the world's crazy and contradictory nature, and proceed gradually to more complicated ones.

Since the advent of Sigmund Freud we know much more about the functioning of the human psyche than we knew before. (By the way, I should like to remark in brackets that there have been five people whose influence was fundamental and who changed humanity's image of itself and the surrounding world: Jesus, Newton, Darwin, Freud and Einstein. As it happens: three Jews and two Englishmen.)

Since Freud we understand the significance of all our seemingly innocent mistakes and verbal slips. The theory is too well-known to be discussed here; and it doesn't matter at all whether the example I am going to give is true (as I was assured) or apocryphal (as I incline to believe). A provincial newspaper, reporting the opening of a garden fête by a well-known and much disliked local figure, announced that the ceremony had been performed "by that battle-scared warrior, Colonel So-and-so". The Colonel was furious and demanded an apology, which duly appeared: "We have to apologise for an unfortunate mistake. We intended, of course, to refer to Colonel So-and-so as 'that bottle-scarred warrior'." We all know that an "unfortunate mistake" is more unfortunate than a plain "mistake" in that it expresses the writer's true opinion although this was the last thing he intended to do.

We have also learnt from Freud that we never forget things we do not mean to forget or which are really important to us. You may forget your wife's birthday but hardly ever your own. We do not spill hot sauce or red wine over a dinner guest unless, at the bottom of our hearts, we mean to hurt him or her. And so on. Innumerable examples could be taken from anybody's everyday life. They are essential parts of our expressing, or at least revealing, ourselves . . . sometimes to ourselves.

This means more than the simple fact that the truth slips out at unguarded moments. It means that mistakes express our true thoughts and feelings while our carefully worded solemn statements do not. The solemn statements are the fruit of careful consideration, tact, self-interest, policy, self-justification or downright dishonesty; the mistakes – the slips of the tongue, the *lapsus linguae* or more appropriately *lipsus languae* – reveal the truth. They represent the revolt of the honest man who is determined to get out of every one of us. It is easy to see what this means: you can trust a man's silly mistakes but you cannot, must not, trust his sincere vows and solemn declarations.

The next step I should like to take is also based on Freud and is closely related to the first but takes matters a little further.

Most people are determined to give the world an idealised picture of themselves. They want to be seen by others (and even more by themselves) not as they are but as they are not. Or as they would like to be. Sometimes they are aware of their weaknesses and wish to hide them; sometimes – perhaps more often – they succeed in hiding the true picture even from themselves. Be that as it may, mean people try to look generous, lazy ones industrious, indolent ones caring and solicitous. When Nietzsche said "If you are going to a woman don't forget your whip" it was because he was a timid man, terrified of women, who never went near them, let alone taking his whip.

13

Moral indignation is the most suspect of all human emotions. Those who hate homosexuals with an uncontrollable fury are only too often suppressed homosexuals; those who wish to hang and flog criminals are either weighed down by guilt and wish to be hanged and flogged themselves – or, just as frequently, have a strong streak of violence in them, like the criminals they want to see flogged, but lack the courage to commit violent crimes, so seek a "legitimate" outlet. This is not my theory, or even Freud's. The Prophet Isaiah declared: "All our Righteousness are as filthy rags." And even the Prophet Isaiah was not all that original.

The greatest fear of all humanity is loneliness and isolation. We are social animals, we must belong to a herd. The herd means acceptance, warmth and some safety. You may join the Punk Rockers, the Skinheads, a criminal gang or White's – it doesn't matter which, but you must *belong*. Swaggering men who display *machismo*, drive fast, talk loudly, wear showy clothes and throw their money about with great ostentation, are, as a rule, poor frightened creatures, crying out for the love and admiration of those whom they pretend to despise. The Nazi and fascist heroes of the thirties (and their descendants today) who goose-step through life with hard-set, terrifying faces are the real cowards. The prophets of doom, the seemingly timid writers, the revolutionary artists, the philosophers who dare to turn against the tide of accepted beliefs – men who dare to be alone – these are the real heroes.

That means that most people are less than meets the eye. It also means that many of us are exactly the opposite of the image we hope to create in the world. You must not believe your eyes.

Let's now take a look into history. It is amazing to observe how many great movements, how many great – or at least important – people have achieved the exact opposite of their aims.

Brutus and company – sincere patriots, most of them –

killed Julius Caesar to prevent tyranny in Rome. Caesar's assassination opened the gates to some of the worst tyrannies the world has ever experienced: the totalitarian madness of Augustus, Tiberius, Nero and Caligula. The French Revolution swept away the Bourbons to put Napoleon on the Imperial throne.

Or a reverse example from more recent times: Austria (with the help of her worst enemy, the Czar) won the Hungarian War of Liberation in 1849. The Austrian triumph was complete. Yet less than twenty years later, at the time of the Crimean War, Austria let down the Czar and gave the Hungarians voluntarily – well, almost voluntarily – much more than they had hoped to gain through two years of desperate struggle.

Hitler is too horrible and too near to us to take a lighthearted view of. Nevertheless, one cannot fail to notice the yawning gap, the chasm between his intentions and his achievements. He meant Germany to rule the world and succeeded in breaking it up into three parts; he was determined to destroy Bolshevism and brought the Soviet Union into the centre of Europe, strengthened it beyond Stalin's wildest dreams, and helped to make it one of the two super-powers; he meant to make the Germans the admired master-race of the world and turned them – for a while – into the most detested and despised race: to use his own phraseology, into the Jews of the world. That Germany has succeeded in shedding this image after his ignominious death, has nothing to do with him. He meant to destroy the Jews and while he carried this intention hideously far, the fact remains that no single individual contributed more to the establishment and immediate recognition of Israel than Adolf Hitler.

Our next step is the consideration of another illusion. All preachers and philosophers, since the dawn of antiquity, have appealed to our better nature. We should love each other, be honest and kind, be peace-loving and nonviolent. Name any virtue and they were in favour of it. Their advice amounted to no more than this: if the world was full of better people, it would be a better world. Pretty obvious, we have all been thinking for the last five thousand years or so. But we were, as usual, mistaken. It is quite possible, indeed likely, that if we had been a nobler and more virtuous breed the earth would be an even more rotten place than it is.

The sad truth is that virtuous and noble intentions have

been responsible for more crimes, wickedness and suffering than any criminal or tyrant has achieved.

Among the earliest murders committed by humanity, there was the murder of innocent people to pacify angry gods: human sacrifice. It is a practice which has continued. Arthur Koestler, in *The Ghost in the Machine*, put it succinctly: "The crimes of Caligula shrink to insignificance, compared to the havoc wrought by Torquemada. The number of robbers, highwaymen, rapers, gangsters and other criminals at any period of history is negligible compared to the massive numbers of those cheerfully slain in the name of true religion, just policy, or correct ideology." He goes on to tell us that it was for the good of their immortal souls that heretics were tortured and burned. Tribal warfare raged not in the interest of the individual but of the tribe, i.e. the common good. Wars of religion were fought to decide fine points of theology, and other sorts of wars – wars of succession, dynastic wars, national and civil wars – were fought for issues in which the fighter had no personal interest whatsoever. The Communists had their "purges" and the very word implies an "act of social hygiene". The gas chambers worked for another kind of hygiene. Adolf Eichmann "was not a monster or a sadist but a conscientious bureaucrat who considered it his duty to carry out his orders."

All this amounts to proof that paradox and madness is not in the beholder's eye but in reality itself. Our mistakes reveal the truth while our well-considered statements often obscure or hide it; people are not at all what they seem to be: the weak are often strong, the hero may be a weakling; the fragile and myopic seeker for the truth is often a real hero; the self-righteous moralist is a crank or a phoney; the men trying to be good caused more pain, suffering and injustice than men trying to be evil; earnest believers in religions and dogmas have caused and are causing more suffering and bloodshed than all the depraved criminals of all the ages put together.

17

Cowardice: a Good Thing

LET US EXAMINE a few more phenomena which are not what they seem to be; or not quite; or indeed – in some cases – are exactly the opposite of what they seem to be.

The word *cowardice* has a pejorative meaning which it often deserves. But even more often it does not. Admittedly, there is nothing particularly admirable in sheer funk, but circumspection, prudence, caution and vigilance, are all cousins of cowardice, and are thoroughly respectable. The other fellow's prudence is cowardice to us, while our own cowardice is always commendable caution, foresight and vigilance.

Cowardice is associated with fear. The idea persists that the coward is afraid and the brave man is not. The man who is not afraid of danger is not a hero but a psychopath. There are some adventurers, psychologically damaged people, who *like* being shot at or putting their lives at risk just for the hell of it. They are not acting bravely: they are simply enjoying themselves. The brave man is the one whose heart sinks into his boots but who stands his ground. The more petrified he is the braver.

People expect a man in military uniform to be heroic, and a man in a police uniform to be pretty brave. The same man in mufti is entitled to tremble. In a recent case two policemen shot an innocent chap mistaking him for an armed criminal. They were put on trial for attempted murder. They put forward the defence that they had been terrified that the other man might shoot first. They were acquitted.

People also maintain that it is horrible cruelty to kill women and children but quite all right to kill the adult male. As an adult (perhaps slightly more than adult) male, I like to believe that to blow up innocent bystanders or people praying in church, or shopping at Harrods, deserves disapproval whatever the age or sex of the victim may be.

Man is the only animal who knows that he is going to die. He cannot bear the idea, so he has invented the immortal soul. He has a soul while animals (i.e. *other* animals) have no soul. The survival of this idea is incongruous in an age which is inclined to believe that we are animals like the rest, even if intellectually – though not morally – more advanced. We can fly to the moon, while bears, elephants, jackdaws and boa constrictors cannot. We are intelligent enough to fly to the moon; they are intelligent enough not to. This ability, however, is a much smaller difference between man and other animals than we like to pretend. I personally find it hard to believe that Hitler and Stalin (and I could name a few personal acquaintances, too) have souls, while my cats Tsi-Tsa and Ginger have not. It may be the other way round. But I don't believe even that.

Religion – every religion – is based on fear: fear of death. So as religion is generally regarded as a Good Thing, cowardice must be a Good Thing, too.

Fear – or call it cowardice – is one of our most useful traits. Without fear, without the instinct of self-preservation, no species could survive. No one could remain alive if he were not a coward to some extent. Let us all turn heroes and the human race will perish. But as the human race is going to perish, in any case, in a few million years if not sooner, this change would not really affect the outcome, only its timing.

Freedom: a Bad Thing

IF THERE IS one noble idea to warm people's hearts, it is Freedom. Utter that word and people's eyes become moist. For freedom men will fight; for freedom they are ready to sacrifice their lives. Millions have died for it – and most of them were cheated. Their deaths (with very few exceptions) achieved nothing. Often they contributed to the very opposite of what was hoped for.

If there was one just war in history; it was World War Two. Mankind really did have to rid itself of the criminal psychopaths ruling Germany, so we and our descendants should be grateful to the Few – and also to the Many – who saved us from a new Dark Age. They were all fighting for freedom . . . or were they? Western Europeans may claim as much, and justly; but the Russians fought just as bravely as they did, and what sort of freedom did their victory bring to them? Stalin's murderous paranoia was horrible enough in the thirties, but after victory was achieved in the name of freedom it became much worse. During the course of history many millions of people have fought heroically for the cause of freedom, against many other millions who have fought just as bravely on the other side – that is to say, for slavery.

And when a group, a clan, a tribe, a class, a nation happens to fight for a just cause, victory does not necess-arily entail the victory of justice. As soon as the battle is won, attitudes change. The victors start defending their newly gained privileges against their former allies, who can become worse off than ever before. The oppressed of yesterday become the new oppressors – as convinced of their natural, often divine, rights as their former oppressors used to be.

All this, you may say, may be true but it does not discredit the noble *idea* of freedom. The sad truth is that humanity, with shining eyes and fast-beating hearts, pays lip-service to freedom, but is afraid of it. Humanity at large does not *want* to achieve freedom. It runs away from it. Freedom means responsibility and people are terrified of responsibility. Freedom – the proper use of freedom – means loneliness (alone-ness as some psychologists call it), and loneliness is the one thing humanity dreads even more than freedom.

People march or fly or drive into battle for their king, their country, their ideas. They die heroes' deaths because they dare not face their fellow men and declare that they do not care a hoot whether Sparta or Athens enjoys the hegemony of the Peleponnese, that it is all the same to them whether the Habsburgs or the Bourbons rule in Spain, or whether Islam is dominant in Bulgaria or not. It is easier to face Spartans, Habsburgs, Bourbons and janissaries than your elders and your brainwashed contemporaries who firmly believe that you must act in the way they wish you to act. (They themselves, as a rule, would not dream of acting at all.) Most of the victims of past wars did not die for freedom. They died because they were afraid of real freedom. They died because they were afraid to say that some causes were not their causes, that they would not derive any benefits either from the Habsburgs or the Bourbons. They preferred dying rather than accepting the responsibility of speaking their minds. Dying is easy; speaking up is very difficult.

The problem is not only that of political freedom. Political freedom is not everybody's main concern. Freedom of worship is not a burning problem for the atheist – or even for the non-practising, vague believer. Lack of freedom of speech does not concern those who have nothing to say or who do not wish to say anything.

But the matter is not quite as simple as that. First – on a rather innocent level – it is like the opera used to be in Australia. There was an old, pre-war refugee joke: two would-be emigrés meet somewhere in Europe and one asks the other where he is off to. "Australia," he is told. He makes a derogatory grimace. "Good God," he says, "to Australia? What a place!" – "Why, what's wrong with Australia?" – "It hasn't even got an opera-house." – "I see . . . Tell me: how often did you go to the opera in the last twenty-five years?" – "Not once, but that's neither here nor there. The point is that I can go if I want to."

The man had a valid point there. There is a world of a difference between not going to the opera in Sydney when there was no opera in Sydney and not going today by your own choice. It is one thing to keep quiet because you have nothing to say and quite another not to be allowed to say what you want. We in the West look down smugly upon the people of Eastern Europe. They are not permitted to express their views, they are forced to compromise throughout their lives and this is soul-destroying, this creates a slave-mentality which undermines the public will more effectively than any Big Brother could undermine it. But, in fact, *they* have every reason to look down upon us. It is one thing to compromise, to hold your tongue because if you rebel, or criticise, or grumble, you endanger your promotion in your job, or your job itself, or you may deprive your child of his chances of getting into a university. Over there you may be angry, frustrated, enslaved but, at least, you know why you are compelled to make a sacrifice. But what about us who are free to say whatever we wish but freely accept the tyranny of society, of public opinion, of employers, of club-mates, of fellow trade-unionists, of neighbours, of experts, of newspapers? We are told that a picture is a Rembrandt, so we admire it;

we are told that a kind of wine is very expensive, so we genuinely enjoy it. We are told what to wear (whether we are society ladies or Punk Rockers), what to eat, what to drink, what to think, so we wear, eat, drink and think those things. Voluntary slavery is more repulsive than enforced slavery.

The explanation confirms what I have already said. Man does not *want* to be free. Half of humanity is stupid and has nothing to say. Very well, to be stupid is a basic human right. But nearly everybody wishes to be a slave of conformism and the right to be a slave is also one of the fundamental human rights.

I gave an example of humanity's inclination towards slavery in an early book of mine, *East is East*: an example which I came across in Siam (as it then was).

Court etiquette there was very strict, and it was held that a servant's head must never be higher than his master's, or a subject's than the King's. As for a servant's or a subject's *feet* – if they were higher than the master's or the King's head, that was sacrilege indeed. For this reason the building of tall houses used to be forbidden in Siam, to ensure that no subject's feet should be higher than the head of the sovereign.

By the time I visited the place these restrictions had been eased, but they were still in force in the presence of the King himself. Royal pages, for example, had to crawl when they were in the royal presence. To crawl properly demanded acrobatic skill. At least one palm had to be flat on the floor, which the page's forehead must also touch. If he happened to be carrying a large tray laden with – say – thirty-two full glasses, his performance became a virtuoso act worthy of any circus.

Crawling was still the rule in the houses of some aristocrats, as well as in the royal palace, but it was becoming rarer. A new generation of enlightened nobles was trying to abolish it. But old habits die hard. A prince of the royal blood told me: "I abolished the practice in my own house long ago – or rather, I tried to abolish it. I told my servants that worms crawled, not human beings."

"They must have been delighted and grateful," I remarked.

He replied that on the contrary, they were resentful. "They are extremely conservative. Much more so than we princes. They believe in my being a prince and their being servants. They *like* crawling. They say they owe me some respect. I told them that I did not see why, but in any case they had to find some other means of expressing their deep respect for me and give up crawling."

"So they gave it up," I nodded. "With regret, maybe, but they gave it up."

"Not at all. They are still trying to get away with it. They crawl less but they still crawl as much as they safely can. They walk up to me with a tray and then, when handing me the drink, they suddenly collapse. They crawl when they think I don't see them. And the amount of crawling that goes on as soon as I am out of the house is almost incredible. In Europe little children start crawling on their own and as soon as they are able to crawl, they are taught how to walk. In my household little children, as soon as they know how to walk, are taught how to crawl. My servants love crawling. They seem to enjoy it. They also believe in it and regard it as their birthright."

I understood. There is a strong desire in the bosom of man to be free; and an equally strong desire to remain a slave; to be told what to do; to crawl.

Luther and Calvin were not the only religious leaders who taught us to humiliate ourselves before the sight of God. All religions have invented God, or Gods, so that people could abase themselves before Him or Them. God is great, while we human beings are worms in the mud, helpless, unworthy and miserable insects. This is the kind of Love of Freedom installed in us at a tender age. Millions of brave people have sacrificed their lives in order to be permitted to remain slaves in their own way and to crawl in the dirt before divine or human masters – according to their hearts' desire.

The Faith of the Unbeliever

JUST ONE FINAL example of blatant contradiction.

A Hell's Angel (to choose one type out of many) thinks he is a man who opts out; he is, in fact, a man who opts in. He has failed, or he fears that he will fail, in conventional society, and he has no doubt that it is society's fault. So he tries an alternative society. He seeks to defy conventional society, says that he despises its rules and narrow outlook but, in fact, he is desperate for approval: the approval of a sect. He does not shave half of his hair off and make a dirty mess of the other half because he deems that hairstyle pretty. He has to do it in order to gain the approval of those who hate doing it just as much as he does but have to do it because, in turn, they seek, *his* approval. He may be a gentle soul, but he must go on the rampage and bash in people's heads because this is the clan's ritual. On such occasions, at least at the beginning, he does not go wild and does not lose control, he simply follows a ritual, just as offering a turn in a pub or singing the Red Flag is the ritual of other gatherings. This is how many sects of non-believers are created all over the world. Poor Hell's Angels! They are trying to persuade themselves that they are strong individualists, defying society; they are lonely babes crying out for mother's love.

We all know the wise saying (which, like many other wise sayings, has become a worn-out cliché) that power corrupts and absolute power corrupts absolutely. But

absolute *lack of power* corrupts even more (if it is possible to corrupt more than absolutely). Every man – the meanest and even the least authoritarian among us – must have *some* power, some influence; must have a dog to kick although – quite rightly and understandably – most people prefer to kick other people rather than dogs. If someone cannot acquire such an inferior for himself as an individual, he will try to obtain him through a group. Perhaps he will feel he is "somebody" because he is white; or because he is a man and not a mere woman; or because he has money; or because he is the descendant of a certain family; or because he is a wild eccentric, different from everyone else. If he becomes – or regards himself as being – a member of a powerful or respected or glamorous group, he shares in its glory. All he has to surrender is his personality and integrity with a large part of his self-respect thrown in. But as he is not likely to have had much of a personality and integrity to start with, the bargain is quite a reasonable one.

But even conformism and non-conformism are slightly more complicated phenomena than we think at first sight.

We are inclined to believe that the man with the balanced views, who has settled down in society, plays his expected part and is "getting on" splendidly is a sane and useful member of society; while the other fellow, who cannot or will not settle down and is constantly rebellious and critical, is a poor neurotic who deserves our pity or condemnation. This is partly true: no society – including the most revolutionary societies – could remain even more or less cohesive if we were all neurotic rebels.

Yet, it is always the critical neurotic who forces society to change and progress. The decent and sane fellow may be approved by the custodians of law and order, he may indeed be "getting on", but he pays a heavy price: he behaves as he is expected to, he is anxious to please and he must sacrifice his personality into the bargain. The neurotic non-conformist may be unhappy, but he is unhappy in his own way and this unhappiness is often more satisfying and relaxing than being happy to order and under pressure.

The Age of Compromise

MOST EIGHTEENTH-CENTURY philosophers firmly believed in Rationalism, which sees in "natural reason" the source of all truth. The history of Rationalism starts with the Stoics and ends with me; and like all history it is chequered and contradictory. Religious rationalists tried to prove all religious teachings and dogmas on purely rational grounds. In other words, Rationalism became such a force that even the irrational could not survive without a rational basis. The fiercest rationalists of pre-revolutionary France were convinced that as soon as people saw the light of clear and irrefutable Reason, the battle would be won. Once people see what is reasonable they cannot help following the obvious course, just as a rabbit cannot help running into the shining light of a reflector. Well, rabbits always make for the light; human beings hardly ever.

Rationalists, like Euclidean geometers, based their case on a few "self-evident truths". But Einstein convinced the world that there was no such thing as a self-evident truth. A few things were self-evident all right; but they were not true. The shortest way between two points is not the straight line; Time and Length are not absolute notions. This seemed to be the death-knell of rationalist philosophy. If there is no self-evident truth, there is no Rationalism. But Rationalism refused to lie down and die. Luckily, Rationalism was not quite as rational as all that.

Paul Johnson has stated that the modern world began on the 29th May 1919 with the photographs taken of a solar eclipse in West Africa and Brazil – the photographs proving that Einstein's theory of relativity was correct. That put many of our previous convictions out of date. We simply had to think anew.

Rationalism ought to have died on the same day. Or, at least, a New Rationalism ought to have been born. But nothing of the sort happened. Philosophers continued their old battles, and as long as there are two philosophers alive the battles will go on with unabated fury and bitterness. Ordinary people either did not realise the significance of the 29th May 1919, or did not care. They discovered a simple and effective solution. They realised (and this is as important a discovery as Einstein's theory – indeed, for ordinary people it is more important) – that Rationalism and Irrationalism may go happily hand in hand, they may co-exist. In fact, they *have* co-existed ever since the days of the Stoics. The truth is even more surprising: they cannot exist without each other.

In the nineteenth century you were either a believer or a non-believer. (In earlier centuries you were either a believer or were burnt at the stake.) The rule of "either/or" is now dead. You are probably a non-believer who will nevertheless have a church-wedding, will have your baby christened and will be buried according to the rites of the religion in which you did not believe. Or you may be a sort of vague believer but find no time to practise your religion and go to church. (Of course, there remains a band of true and sincere believers but their number keeps shrinking.)

In the old days you were either a Tory or a Liberal; later, a Tory, a Liberal or a Labour-party follower. But ours is the Age of the Floating Voter. People change their allegiance for the most trivial and frivolous reasons, from election to election, and back again. People change their allegiance almost as light-heartedly as some parties change their programmes.

In many cases people *see* reason but – whatever the eighteenth-century Rationalists said – fail to follow it. They know perfectly well that to judge a man by the colour of his skin is downright stupid, but they go on making such judgments. They know perfectly well that to revere a man because he is an aristocrat or a member of the royal family is plain silly, but they will go on bowing their heads and breathing heavily in the presence of such a person.

Seeing the irrationality of a belief does not mean that people can – or will even try to – get rid of it. They form various kinds of community to forward their own interests: clubs, a society of snooker-players, or a nation. A state, logically, is not more than a society to promote common interests and provide protection. Yet, while people would not consider sacrificing their lives for their borough, their local library or their bowling club, they are ready to die for the state. In pure logic the state should not be more sacred than the bowling club.

Lest my readers believe that I am sitting here in judgment over other people and trying to speak as the supreme rationalist, I hasten to assure them that this is not the case. I believe in the idea that a country is no more than a Mutual Protection Society and yet I am a great British patriot, with the extra fervour of the convert added to my natural zeal. But at least I am fully aware of the weakness of my so-called Rationalism, the contradictions between my theory and practice. And this is a good thing. Confusion and contradiction have always served humanity better than clear, cold logic.

I used to be a firm enemy of religion. I put all religious feelings down to cowardice and was proud of my own courage in having discarded belief in Hell and Heaven, in the immortal soul, in Creation, in the Trinity, in miracles, in saints and in various other fairy tales, as they seemed to me. I disliked all priests and agreed with my step-father who often remarked that being a priest was no profession for a man. (Nuns were all right.) By now I have learnt that I was wrong and I have become – like the whole of Europe – more tolerant.

Religion may be based on cowardice, but it is a necessity, a basic human need. Being such weak and fallible creatures, why should we not comfort ourselves? Indeed, we have to. Religion may be a bunch of fairy tales but fairy tales, too, are basic necessities. Religion may be bunk but it makes many people more understanding, wiser, more tolerant, more broad-minded and happier than they would be without it. It gives meaning to many lives and as we are reluctant to accept the idea that life has no special meaning, we should be grateful for the gift.

All churches comprise many people, from the wicked to the good. There are the mad bigots of the Ayatollah Khomeini type, there are the hypocrites who make a good living as workers in the church industry and there are, of course, the honest believers – priests and laymen – for whom religion is the true meaning of life. But it is not the true believers who keep the churches powerful; it is the vast army of non-believers who help to preserve the churches' strength. Religions may be true or untrue – as they contradict one another they cannot all be true. But the *need* for religious belief is certainly real for many people.

I believe in Pure Logic. I believe in the Sanctity of Reason. I loathe all superstition. I walk under ladders and do not mind starting any important enterprise on a Friday the thirteenth. But I always knock on wood. Knocking on wood is an intelligent and reasonable precaution, it has nothing to do with superstition.

The great compromise between Reason and Irrationality has been the *de facto* rule of our lives for many a century; why not acknowledge it, *de iure*, as a Good Thing and put Confusion and Contradiction on the pedestal they deserve?

It is the sign of a strong character to stick to principles and beliefs through thick and thin. I admire such characters and wish I were one of them. If someone wishes to believe that God created humanity as the crowning glory

of the universe, if he wishes to believe that nothing matters in those many thousand million years through which the Universe existed than those two million or so years during which a species which calls itself *Homo sapiens* has graced and will continue to grace (or disgrace) a provincial planet, let him do so. Particularly as those *Homines sapientes* are *us*; that provincial little planet is *ours*; and that the time *we* are living in is (if we are lucky and less stupid than seems probable) just about the middle of that brief moment in Eternity, *our* two million years.

On Low-Brow Happiness

MAN HAS INVENTED many ways of escaping freedom and the responsibility that goes with it. One of the commonest methods is to conform. Sometimes, as we have seen, people conform with the rules of a small, even eccentric, clique, in an attempt to have it both ways: to look like a rebel while being a conformist.

It has always been a tricky job to keep the masses down and see to it that the few should be able to run the lives of the many (which is, in fact, the story of humanity). It was easier in feudal times when people accepted – had to accept – the place in society allocated to them by their birth. You could not move up or down in society and that was that. It did not even occur to you that this eternal law might change. But change it did, with Capitalism. The acquisition of money, or the loss of it, became something that could change your status. Money ruled cruelly and firmly but mobility became possible, so the privileged rich – and other rulers – had to rely more and more on persuasion. An important factor was and is the power of snobbery, which is one of the most powerful motivating factors of mankind.

We are told what to do and what not to do, what to believe and what not to believe, and everyone – well, almost everyone – obeys the rules. We are told that an ancient Greek torso is a masterpiece, so generation after generation of us sincerely admire it, even though it may be nothing special in the way of sculpture. We are told that an idiotic but fashionable play is uproariously funny and we go along and *genuinely* enjoy it, even if there remains a lingering doubt at the bottom of our hearts that we have really been bored to tears. We are told that people of taste drink dry wine only, and we dare not admit that we really like sweet wine. (As a French vinegrower told me contemptuously: "The English like their wine dry as long as it is sweet enough.") A few decades ago it was decided that a serviette must be called a napkin: that anyone who called a serviette a serviette disclosed the fact that he was not of aristocratic origin or did not mix with aristocrats. As no sales-manager, no full partner in a solicitors' firm and no ambitious junior executive is ready to admit that he does not belong to the upper crust, all such people would rather bite their tongues off than utter the word *serviette*. I have heard of a man whose last word – uttered with his last breath – was "serviette". He had always longed to utter it at least once, but he knew he could not survive it. He didn't.

Another important rule of snobbery is that you must find life unbearable and look into the future with horror however happy your natural disposition may be. To be happy and content with life, to be an optimist, is irrefutable evidence of being a superficial fool, a shallow and insensitive idiot. It is the most low-brow of all attitudes. Many naturally jolly and convivial men, without a worry in the world, strive desperately hard to learn how to be miserable and utter gloomy prophecies about the future of mankind. (The increase of crime, deterioration of manners, disrespect for the old, vandalism, football hooliganism, rising prices, police brutality *and* the decrease of respect for the police are all reasonably good to be inconsolable about.) If the intellectual snobs are not to see you as a despicable, low-brow half-wit, you must collapse at least twice a day under the weight of a hopeless present and even darker future.

The arguments of the gloom-mongers are based on two main premises.

1. *Wherever you look, you see misery, civil wars, starvation, nuclear rearmament, tyranny and selfishness.* If they looked around a little more carefully, they would also see happiness, well-being, peace, democracy and unselfishness, but they do not wish to see anything of the kind. Further: they genuinely believe that their noble souls are being upset by the state of the world. But let me tell you loudly, clearly and unequivocally: *no man has ever been unhappy because of public affairs.* A man may be arrested by a tyrannical regime and that will make him pretty miserable; but in this case tyranny has become his private affair. What I mean is this: if you live in South Kensington (or Ealing, or Chester) you will not be unhappy and depressed because of the civil war in San Salvador. You may be concerned and outraged; you may feel that you ought to do something – and, indeed, you may even do something. But if you think that you *feel depressed* because of the civil war in San Salvador you are wrong: the depression is *simply your own depression* which you are projecting onto the civil war.

2. The other argument is this: *how can you enjoy yourself when the world is preparing itself for self-destruction? When we are all going to be blown up in one second, or live perhaps a few more days in a radio-active desert?*

To my mind, if this premise is true, it is a convincing argument for trying to enjoy yourself in happy abandon. Even a man who is being executed the following morning gets a good supper and a drink the night before – the idea being that he should have a few pleasant moments before he is dispatched to eternity. But there is another answer too. By all means, do whatever you can to avoid a nuclear disaster. Follow your conscience, join the CND or fight the CND, whatever your inclination bids you to do. On the other hand this nuclear threat has been hanging over us since 1945 and it needs a tremendous capacity for despondency not to have smiled, laughed, enjoyed a good meal and lovely company, beautiful pictures, exciting books, breathtaking scenery for forty years. Even the

gloomiest gloom-mongers must have slipped up occasionally and enjoyed a good cigar, and smiled – however vaguely – at a good joke. And if *one* cigar and *one* smile are permissible, why not ten? Or ten thousand? That's not so many during forty years. This attitude, once again, is a projection of your personal dejection and gloom, and also of your laziness. It is a wonderful excuse for not doing anything, for sitting about in a state of luxurious misery while all those happy-go-lucky, insensitive fools get on with the work.

The profound question – uttered with a knowing sigh – is this: "*How can I busy myself with trivialities when the bomb of Damocles is hanging over my head?*" But the bomb does not keep you *busy*. You can do your job to the last second. All you have to do in that last second is to blow up.

When I was still a journalist in Budapest, someone told me that two brothers, who owned a cinema, were rather dispirited because business was bad. They went to have a peep at the auditorium to see what sort of house there was. One came back depressed, and declared: "The house is half empty." The other was radiant: "The house is half full!"

The story may be apocryphal but that is not the point. The point is that both reports were true, yet they were each other's opposite. This is certainly a basic division of humanity: the half for whom the cinema is half empty and the other half for whom it is half full.

It is quite wrong to say that it is easy to be happy and content when your circumstances are rosy. Your contentment has very little – indeed, nothing – to do with your circumstances. The two cinema-owning brothers shared the same circumstances. (True, one was the elder brother, so he had a different position in the family which may have coloured his whole outlook . . . perhaps. But let us not get involved here in the labyrinths of Freudian – or Adlerian – psychology.) We can see daily plenty of examples of people envied by everyone, who ought to be as happy as can be, and who are in fact miserable. This very day the papers reported the story of one of the most famous "super-stars", the darling of the gossip-columns, who has had to be taken to hospital to be cured of drug-addiction.

At the other end of the scale, who has not met the cheerful beggar, the person who can take a series of misfortunes in his stride, who is unbroken by adversity and amusing about his own bankruptcy, or bad health, or the elopement of his wife with his best friend?

All events, and even disasters, do have a sunny side – or at least some lurking advantage. The blessing may be disguised (as Churchill once remarked) very successfully, but it is always there. The trouble is more people can see the gloom in good luck than can see the rosy side of disasters.

When I was told in 1977 that I was going blind, I was not really overjoyed. If I had been offered a choice I would have said that I would rather keep my eyesight. Indeed, for a while, for the first time in my life, I considered whether it would not be better to commit suicide. I weighed the pros and cons as unemotionally as anyone can, when considering his own demise. I had had a long and pleasant life, so why should I add a few miserable years to the happy ones and be a burden on others? Then I started to notice brave and wise blind people who were leading a full life and I began, slowly, to see some advantages in going blind in one's sixties. It was a challenge, I decided: to overcome a disability and remain not just a person, but a happy and cheerful person. And what about music? I had neglected music all my life. It had meant little to me until my more advanced years, when I started enjoying it more and more discovering beauties I had missed previously. In my younger days I sang horribly out of tune (but with great gusto and enthusiasm); the gusto and enthusiasm remained with me but my ear improved year by year. Now would be the time, I thought, to enrich my life in a way I had never thought possible, while, inevitably, it would be impoverished in many other ways. I cannot claim to have been disappointed when I did not go blind but I do claim to have been quite ready for the event and to have seen the consoling side of blindness, too.

What could be more terrible, degrading and destructive than being a prisoner at Auschwitz?

After the war many friends and acquaintances – and some complete strangers – visited me in London and told me harrowing stories about the camp. I took one of my visitors to the Hungarian *Csárda* – an excellent restaurant in those days – and he told me his story. Not only did he, like everyone else in Auschwitz, have to live with death day by day, but on one occasion he was actually taken into the gas chamber and let out again at the last minute, before the gas was switched on to kill all the others in the chamber. He told me that he regarded the rest of his life as a present, an odd gift. He was satisfied with everything that came his way, anyone could kick him around – he didn't care. No blow in life was a real blow after Auschwitz, and every pleasure, however tiny, was manna from Heaven.

A fortnight later I went to the *Csárda* again. As I arrived too early for my appointment I went down to the bar and waited, sipping a drink. Then, suddenly, I heard a quarrel upstairs. A customer was reproaching the proprietor – bitterly and rather rudely – for not giving him a corner table although he had booked three days before. The proprietor pleaded some excuse, but it was rejected: the man insisted on a corner table and he got it in the end. While the quarrel was going on I gradually recognised the voice of my Auschwitz friend.

The moral of this tale is not that the man was a poseur, a liar, or inconsistent. He had been absolutely sincere when he was talking to me a fortnight earlier. The moral is that, having gone through the most devastating and humiliating experience life could inflict upon a man, he was a healthy and strong enough character to regain his self-respect, his will to live and his necessary dose of arrogance. Having survived, he was entitled to the corner tables of this life like everybody else. Perhaps even a little more.

The simple truth is that life is what you make of it. Life is there to be lived. The art of living is not an easy art but surely it is the most important and most generally practised of all arts. True, some people are luckier than others but the happy ones are not always the lucky ones. There is no life which does not offer pleasure, beauty, a wonderful challenge and ample rewards – if you know how to grab your opportunities. Many people try to learn to paint, to write and hundreds of other major and minor skills but they do not even try to learn to live. They accept the Commandment of the Bores: "Thou shalt be gloomy." To hell with the Gloom-Mongers and Bores. Life is beautiful, funny, amusing, varied, colourful, exciting and enjoyable. One *can* learn how to be happy.

Yes, yes – I hear the voice of some impatient reader – it is all too easy for you to say this. But you just tell me *how* to enjoy this horrible, depressing mess, called life.

I am afraid I cannot teach you "How to be happy" in one easy lesson. Not even in ten. But I can give you two basic rules.

1. It is a question of determination. You must liberate yourself from the tyranny of fashion which hammers into everbody's head that life is unbearable. Once you accept the fundamental thesis – the fundamental truth – that life is a joy, a unique gift, that life is some sort of an ore: you must discard what is useless and get to the real treasure, then you are half way there.

2. Do not give up your dreams and ambitions. Do not be modest. Reach out for the moon, by all means, if that is your inclination. It is a gamble and you may win. But he is a foolish gambler who is not aware of the possibility of losing. Or just winning a tiny sum. When you look at your

life, remember: the art is not to achieve a lot – to win a vast and fabulous fortune – but to be content with what you have – whatever that may be.

Millions of people spend their lives pondering over the question: is there life after death? They do not even consider the simpler and more relevant problem: is there life *before* death? There is.

Part Two: Particular Wisdom

How to be Born

THIS IS ONE of the most important decisions of your life.

First of all you have to decide whether you want to be born at all. To take the plunge into life is a risky business. The unborn are safe. In fact, only the unborn are safe. They are in an enviable position: they don't have to worry about anything; they have no financial or health problems; they never become unemployed. Being born entails the inevitability of death. Only the unborn are immortal. Not in the sense that their life will go on forever – as it has not even begun – but immortal in the sense that they will never die. True, they do not have much fun – this is something they share with the Gloom Mongers and the higher intellectuals.

The Unborn are also much more numerous than the Born. They outnumber us by millions to one. I shudder to think of a conflict between *them* and *us*. It is our great good luck that they are so badly organised.

But if in spite of all my warnings you decide to take the more adventurous course, then you must decide *when* you want to be born. About three-quarters of the people who play "When would you like to have lived?" choose Periclean Athens. This is an extremely unwise choice. Yes, of course, the intimacy of the city state, its fermenting, effervescent cultural life, its model democracy are all attractive. Pericles made Athens great. But there were snags, only too often forgotten. We all remember Athenian democracy, but tend to forget the Delian League, an instrument of Athenian despotic imperialism. We

all remember that Pericles made Athens great, but tend to forget that he also made it small. He was responsible for the Peleponnesian War which was supposed to undo Persia but undid Athens instead. Then there was the plague – and Pericles was eventually deprived of all his honour and sentenced (fined only) as a sort of early war criminal (it is true that he was later reinstated, with apologies). In spite of all this, most people insist that they would have loved to live in the Periclean era. They all presume, of course, that they would have been friends of Pericles, would have studied under Zeno and Anaxagoras, would have been constant visitors to the studios of Phidias and Callicrates and would have watched the building of the Parthenon. No one sees himself as a slave in that wonderful Athenian democracy, although there were many more slaves about than personal friends of

Pericles. Not one of those dreamers has ever declared that he or she would fancy dying of the plague.

And there is another important point to be remembered. Plague or no plague, slaves or free men, rich or poor, artists or warriors, all those citizens of Periclean Athens have been dead for nearly two and a half thousand years. I see no beauty or pleasure in being dead half that time.

If you do make the brave decision to be born, take my advice and be born in the future, not in the past.

What sort of family should you choose? A difficult question, worthy of careful consideration.

The first idea which comes to the mind of many of my readers is that they would be inclined to choose a rich family. Rich families *can* be a good choice, but rarely are. I cannot possibly deny my prejudice against the rich as countless millions have read my book *How to be Poor* (a few odd copies are still available). I made it clear that to my mind respectable middle-class poverty is the ideal existence, riches are a curse. Rich children – even today – are often brought up by nannies or other "staff" who may be better influences than their mothers – but this makes matters even worse. Rich parents, to make up for their neglect, spoil their children, not realising that a spoilt child is a kind of battered child – often more helpless than a battered child in the literal sense, because not so tough.

If you are an avid reader of George Orwell – and who isn't nowadays? – and have been infected by his romantic admiration of the proletariat, you might hesitate and ask yourself whether you should be born in a proletarian family. Your difficulty will be to find a proletarian family. The very word "proletarian" has gone out of fashion (the proud "proletarian" as well as the contemptuous "prole") both here, in the decadent West and also in the East of Europe where the proletarians are supposed to rule. "Comrade" – well, if you must; "proletarian" – never!

47

Quite a few families with cars, colour TV, washing-machines and holidays in Spain still try posing as pro-letarians, but they are not too convincing. Belonging to the working class – that is still possible, although only just – does not mean that you are a struggling prole, a poor and deprived man, just as belonging to the middle class does not mean that you must be reasonably well off. Being unemployed does not make you a proletarian; and being a Trade Unionist does not make you a Labour voter. The working class are trying to do – quite successfully – two things at one and the same time: to despise the middle classes and to join them. What I remarked once before is still true: Britain is the country where the ruling class does not rule, the working class does not work and the middle class is not in the middle.

So what are you to do? My advice is this: forget about class and money. This may be difficult for an Englishman (or woman), even for an unborn Englishman. But try. *Choose your parents well*, as human beings, this is the most important matter for your future happiness, sanity and ability to get on in life.

Your parents need not be rich; they need not be poor; they need not be well educated. They ought not to be too tidy, too pious, too methodical or too anything. They should be reasonably well balanced, happy people who love you in the right way, and you will be perfectly all right. They do not need to consult books on how to bring up babies; they do not even need to keep regular hours in feeding you. They should not be over-anxious, worried or hysterical, they should not shout at you at one moment and cover you with kisses the next. They may even be strict, so long as they are fair and loving. They must not think that the whole world will collapse if you don't eat all your semolina and that they will never recover if you keep them awake during one night. If you are treated with common sense, love and a twinkle in your parents' eyes you will grow into a secure person, you will feel at home in life, you will be trusted and trusting – and that is worth more than any fortune you might inherit.

I was – and still am – deeply impressed by my own daughter, Judy. She is treating her two sons, Alex (aged nearly three) and Harry (aged five months) extremely sensibly. She follows the above rules which means that she follows no rules at all, except the dictates of common sense. The children are perfectly happy and content. What is even more amazing: Alex does not seem to resent Harry and harbour murderous intentions against him, in spite of the fact that Harry dethroned him and deprived him of his position at the centre of the family. Alex is treated with a great deal of love and affection and is taught to treat his little brother in the same way, and to be a "big boy" to protect him.

How does my daughter do it? I have no idea. Perhaps she, too, chose her parents well. Whatever the reason, I cannot possibly say that this is the solution of the problem for *all* children and that all children to be born should be the children of my daughter, Judy. That would be impractical. But do look for a mother like her.

On Childishness

"THE CHILD IS the father of the man," says the old adage, and it creates a puzzle: how can those lovely fathers beget such abominable offspring? Children – most children – are intelligent, lively, sincere, innocent, natural, truthful and loyal; it is education that turns them into stupid, apathetic, competitive and treacherous liars. As education is compulsory, the result is almost inevitable.

The very word "childish" is misapplied. The word ought to mean: intelligent, lively etc etc – see above. But we use it to mean immature, unsophisticated and "improper for a grown-up person". The boot is on the wrong foot: it would be improper to honour most grown-up persons by the adjective, "childish". The word "child-like", it's true, is trying to make amends and means "having the good qualities of a child", but this, too, is a condescending word.

The word "childish" is misleading also in another and even more important sense. It suggests that grown-ups behave as adults *should* while children are an inferior species. This is either a mistake or a downright lie. Adults, on the whole, are more childish than children.

We know that the trouble with humanity (one of the many troubles) is that while its intellect has grown quickly and impressively its morality and ethics are those of the cave-dweller or the crocodile. Man is able to create admirable devices and then uses them for destructive ends. The sciences have opened up glorious vistas but man keeps reverting to murder, terrorism and gangster-ism. Man has remained the slave of base instincts such as revenge, envy, fury, vanity, and what is true of the species is also true of the individual. It is true that a boy of four has to learn a lot – when was the Norman Conquest, what is the capital of Venezuela and how to find the square root of 16 without the help of a pocket calculator – but as far as ethics are concerned he can teach adults a lot.

Children are more serious, too. When I go to play tennis at Hurlingham Club, I very often see small children waiting patiently outside the tennis courts while their parents are playing with a ball. And how often parents shove children to bed much too early in order to be able to start playing bridge as soon as possible. The other day I heard a man scolding his eleven year old boy for showing off and a few hours later making an hysterical scene in the office, abusing his partners and ending up practically in

51

tears – because, in order to save money, they meant to exchange his office Mercedes for a Vauxhall Cavalier. When children play King or Queen, they are fully aware, of pretending; whereas a man spends sleepless nights fretting about whether he will get a knighthood, or some silly letters to put after his name, and when he does, he believes that he *is* a real knight in shining armour. The few who become kings are inclined to believe in their own divinity, and this belief is shared by millions of their subjects who – at the same time – try to teach their children to use their common sense and be realistic.

Adults believe that their work is important while childish problems are . . . well, just childish problems. The truth is exactly the opposite. Admittedly, a number of people are engaged in keeping society going and that may be regarded as important. But most people are engaged in ridiculous pursuits: making a little more money, doing their best to be able to move into a larger house in a so-called better district, driving a larger and faster car, mixing with dull people whose names keep appearing in the gossip columns of the gutter press, pulling a fast one on a business associate and so on. On a different level they fight for the "true religion" and, like the Ayatollah, kill thousands in the process without blinking an eyelid; start rioting in Quebec because they insist that street names must be written up in French in Vancouver, where not a soul speaks French; or blow off people's limbs and blind them because a stretch of land must belong to this country instead of that one. They hijack planes and kill diplomats in order to "draw attention" to some cause. These immature activities are regarded as behaviour worthy of dedicated adults.

When little Alistair wants blue marbles instead of yellow ones (exactly the same marbles as Bruce has) *that* is a truly serious matter. When Alistair is denied those marbles – without adequate reason and without a proper explanation – that is something decisively important.

This will be a formative influence and will partly decide whether little Alistair grows up into a happy, fair-minded member of society or becomes a neurotic, vain Mercedes-chaser, a snob, a terrorist or an Ayatollah.

How old are you? This is a pointless question. Few people know how old they really are. Every person has two ages: the first is their Calendar Age (CA) which is the less important of the two and depends simply on the date of birth. (Its chief purpose is to tell you when you must go to school and whether you are permitted to watch porno-graphic films in public, or must still watch them at home.) The second age is your Real Age (RA), and that is of real importance. After about four (CA), you develop your RA. Your CA changes, making you a year older at every birthday; your RA remains constant. We all know serious-minded, mature human beings with a CA of eleven; and also empty-headed, silly, sulking, vain children with a CA of fifty-four.

The figure of fifty-four, which I jotted down at random, reminds me of an awful story about myself. When I was CA forty-eight my sister – a medical doctor – wanted to give me an injection to prevent me from developing the 'flu. I had just arrived in America and she thought – noticing some symptoms – that I did not want to spend my visit there in bed. I hate injections and hid myself behind a curtain while she went out for her syringe and penicillin (or whatever). After a short search she found me, but then I fled. She pursued me with the syringe in her hand, at the ready. When the battle was over (she won), she asked me: "At what age does a man grow up?" – "Fifty-four," I replied. She said nothing, but six years later she reverted to the subject and told me that I had been over-optimistic. "We must go on waiting," she declared sadly.

There are aged children, elderly toddlers. I had a dear

friend who was seventy-three all his life, until he died at the age of sixty-seven. Twenty-three is a good RA: it is a hopeful, active, forward-looking age. An elderly, fat, pink-faced company director of seven is less attractive.

I find my own theory about the Two Ages of Man so convincing that I started worrying about my own RA. A quick opinion poll among my close friends voted that my Real Age is twelve. Not a splendid verdict for the intellect of a self-appointed sage, but flattering for his character.

On Professional Deformities

No one becomes a hangman by chance, just because there is a job going and – well, one has to live, and it really doesn't matter whether one is a bee-keeper or a public executioner. A gardener may become either a potato-grower or a specialist in roses "just by chance"; a barrister may become an expert on insurance or on criminal cases (they are often closely related); but no one becomes a hangman because it is "just another job".

Hanging, as most of us know, was abolished in Britain about fifteen years ago, so as far as this country is concerned I am speaking of the past. A man may become a hangman because he is convinced that executing a murderer is the right thing to do, and is therefore pleased to offer himself as an instrument of divine, or terrestrial, justice. Or he may become a hangman because he is a sadist who enjoys hanging people and has deluded himself with the above notion of divine, or terrestrial, justice. Or he may become a hangman – and this is the most common reason – because he is a sadist who enjoys hanging people, without any excuse or rationalisation.

Something of this also used to apply to judges. Many of them abhorred capital punishment and tried capital cases with the utmost dismay, while a few barristers even refused judicial appointment lest they should be compelled to put on the black cap. But there were a few who relished the idea of sending people to the gallows and felt deprived when a murderer was reprieved. (You may ask how I know this, since one cannot look into another person's mind. To which I answer: of course one can.)

It was not that judges were, or are, sadists. Very few of them are. But sooner or later most of them develop a God-complex. When everyone keeps kowtowing to you; when people laugh at your silliest jokes and listen to your most trivial utterances as though they were the Sermon on the Mount; when the outcome of quarrels and arguments, and often the fates of men and women and their children, rest in your hands; when you cannot be sacked from your job however incompetent or senile you become . . . when, in other words, you are treated like God, then it is difficult not to believe in your own divinity. You are addressed as "my Lord", almost like Him, so naturally you are inclined to believe that He is your colleague. I should point out, however, that this rule, like all rules, lacks universal validity. I have known cunning geese. I have met naïve foxes. And I have known modest and almost human judges.

Physicians suffer from another kind of professional deformity (PD). That quite a few of them are lazy, that they dislike being dragged out of bed in the middle of the night and care more about themselves than about their patients – these are just human traits, not specifically medical ones. It is Sphynx-like Secrecy which is their PD. They are the Knowers of Secrets, and they hate to divulge them to ordinary people, known as patients. It is not the patient's business to know what is wrong with him. His job is to suffer (which is what is meant by the Latin word *patiens*), and to get better in response to treatment. The doctor's job is to exercise power over life and death. The doctor has been studying for years and years and, at the bottom of his heart, he is aware that he knows very little. So how can the patient expect to know anything? There is a sound division of labour here: the patient doing the suffering, the doctor doing the curing. It is true that if the doctor fails to cure, it is the patient, not the doctor, who dies, but this is in the nature of things (not that the doctor

56

is too keen to change it). But even Nature's rules have no universal validity. Many patients turn to other sources and learn a great deal about their illnesses, becoming – to all intents and purposes – doctors. And sooner or later *all* doctors become patients.

As we have seen from Law and Medicine, the fact that a profession is noble does not make it immune to PDs. Take teaching, for another example. One may become a teacher because one loves children, or because one is a paedophile; and there is danger lurking even for the teacher who chooses his calling because he genuinely believes that educating the young is one of the most useful activities anyone can be engaged in.

If you are the one adult among children – especially among small ones – your cleverness, knowledge and superiority are not questioned. There will occur breaches of discipline, of course, but they will resemble blasphemy. You are not among equals who can demolish your arguments or expose your ignorance, but among naughty children who rebel against your ultimately unchallengeable authority. The blasphemous child, even if positively loutish, is in the final analysis a true believer at heart – a challenger of authority recognizes authority's existence and may even stand in awe before it. Teachers often become teachers, whether they are aware of it or not, because they are anxious to avoid competition with their equals. It is an even simpler and easier way of establishing one's divinity than the way of the judge and the doctor.

Priests, ministers, rabbis, imams and so on – do they have a God-complex too? Indeed they do, of the worst kind. They are God's chums, His representatives on earth. Their humility may be genuine enough – or it may be like Luther's. It may mean "It is only Almighty God before whom I bow my head, and no one else." Luther's humility was the worst kind of arrogance.

I could go on almost indefinitely pointing out the God-complexes of those whose jobs give them power over other

57

people. So do I believe that everyone, or almost everyone, suffers from this complex? That we all carry within us the bug of divinity? I would reply that we are all seekers after God, and many of us hope to find Him in ourselves.

There are innumerable lesser PDs, such as the pomposity of barristers, the literal minds of bureaucrats, the desperate desire to please of actors, the determined avoidance of responsibility of civil servants, the habit of saying nothing in long and unintelligible sentences of academics, the insistence on treating everything as raw material for a book of writers, the brashness and dishonesty of politicians, and the cowardice of humorists who try to hide behind their own jokes. I haven't the space to discuss them all here, but there are two important points which I would like to make.

Do PDs develop during the practice of your trade, or do you choose your trade because of an initial inclination towards its DP? A bit of both, I think: there is probably interaction. You may have a touch of sadism in you when you become a policeman, and then one of two things can happen: either you act out your sadism and enjoy yourself at the expense of your powerless victims, or – while the possession of power pleases you – you learn to control your sadism and to act justly. In the latter case you will still enjoy yourself, but in a constructive manner.

The rule is simple: noble professions remain noble, but beware of their inherent dangers.

The second point this old Guru wants to make is this: whatever your job may be, however noble or however humble, try to enjoy it. Can anyone enjoy routine drudgery day after day? I certainly would not deny that jobs exist which ought not to be done by anybody; but if you are trapped in one of these it is still possible, with determination and practice, to find at least some enjoyment in it. Suppose, for instance, you are a waiter. You may be morose by nature and feel that it's grossly unjust that you have to perform such lowly duties, serving a lot of rich nonentities who are no better than you. You may hate the long walk between kitchen and tables; you may hate accepting tips; you may hate everything and everybody connected with the job. You don't want to lose your job so you make an effort to be as polite as decency demands, but your hatred, dissatisfaction and contempt will show through. It would be far better to convince yourself that your job is one of endless variety, as many waiters believe in any case. Every customer is different from all other customers, but they all appreciate a smile, readiness to please, a little true courtesy and even an apt and friendly joke. The point is not that such an attitude is nicer for the customer: it is nicer for you. A little good humour will not only lengthen your life, but will also increase your income for the same amount of work – or less.

My brother once told me that a waiter who had spilt wine on his jacket and had apologised politely, said as he was wiping it off: "Luckily, sir, it was a very dry wine ..."

A reasonably good joke, which I suspect he was not making for the first time. He may even have spilt the wine on my brother, and on others before him, in order to be able to make it. But that doesn't matter. He was enjoying himself. And so he should.

On Sex

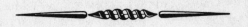

I DO NOT WANT to revert at any length to the old chestnut of hot-water bottles, but I must mention it *en passant*. I have learnt by now that I shall never live down the remark made in *How to be an Alien* (nearly forty years ago) that "Continental people have sex, the English have hot-water bottles". In the sixties, when Kings Road and Carnaby Street were the centre of the universe – people felt that Britain had become the fashion-, pop- and sex-capital of the world. In those days I was often asked ironically: "Well, do we still only have hot-water bottles?" I replied truthfully and not at all ironically: "No. You have certainly progressed. Now you have electric blankets." What I meant is this: Britain has become a copulating country but not an erotic one. The race is maintained and sex – from healthy animal sex down to pornography and, more recently, to video nasties – has become more fashionable, more of a pastime than it was forty years ago. But the alluring, sex-charged, electric atmosphere of, say, Italy is still light-years away. I am not particularly fond of wolf-whistles but those women between the ages of nine and ninety who complain about it on their return from Italy – they are extremely fond of them. Occasionally they are genuinely annoyed but, on the whole, the wolf-whistle makes them feel wanted, and attractive, and they are reminded of the fact that they are women (which in many cases they are not yet or are not any more).

I have just learnt from the pen of Germaine Greer that

sex is, once again, out of fashion. When such an impressive female Guru makes such an egregious, indeed momentous declaration, most people are inclined to believe her. Ms Greer goes as far as to recommend chastity as a Good Thing. I have a vague feeling that she has joined the Tolstoy-Muggeridge Axis. I am always a little suspicious when male roués are converted to chastity in their old age. I do not doubt that they are sincere, but there is a lingering doubt in my nasty mind about the cause of their sincerity: can it be that as they cannot enjoy sex any more, they try to persuade humanity to give it up too? Absolute integrity and subconscious desire may, of course, go hand in hand. I personally may have – if I am lucky – a few more years before I am converted to such noble ideas. I paraphrase St Augustine's famous prayer: "Oh God, do not give me chastity, please keep it from me as long as possible."

Chastity does not threaten us yet on any wide scale. The real trouble with sex in this country is that it has become a social and political game. Sex occasionally intrudes into high politics (remember Profumo, Parkinson, etc) but, as a rule, it is the other way round: it is not sex that intrudes into politics but politics that dominate sex.

Let us deal with the social aspect of the question first. Britain is not and will never be the land of the wolf-whistle. Video-nasties, yes; rape, too often; filthy magazines, yes. But wolf-whistles: never. The English (perhaps not all the British but the English) are too cool, too reserved, too well-mannered for that. In the old days you asked a woman: "Will you come home with me and see my etchings?" Today you forget about the etchings but ask the same matter-of-fact question. More reticent people may mention a night-cap, even today. If the answer to this question is *yes*, it is fine; if it is *no*, it is equally fine. You know where you are. You may ask other ladies at the same party and sooner or later one will say *yes*. It does not really matter which lady. A few girls do not regard a party as a success if they have to return home after it to sleep in their own beds. It does not really matter whose bed it is as long as it is not theirs. This is all very straightforward and honest, even if it is not very romantic.

Another change in the social climate of sex in the post-hot-water-bottle era has been that such antiquated ideas as jealousy and fidelity are allegedly going out of fashion. To regard a woman as your own property (that is how jealousy and fidelity have been interpreted) is an insult which offends against all feminist principles. A *man's* right to philander has never been seriously questioned throughout the ages. Female infidelity was always regarded as an outrage, in some societies punishable by death. (It is not so very long ago that a Queen of England – wife of the worst royal rake – died on the scaffold because of alleged unfaithfulness.) At the same time, all over the

THE UNFAITHFULL WIFE
VICTORIAN SCHOOL

world, while they were stoning women to death for their infidelity, male philandering was regarded as a bit of a joke. A chap must have a bit of fun. Ferenc Deák, a Hungarian statesmen and guru of the last century, explained this discrepancy, though in terms which were rather inelegant. He said: "There is a lot of difference between stepping in shit with my boots on, and someone shitting into my boots." Little wonder that post-World Wars generations have revolted against such male chauvinist piggery.

There have been several attempts at solutions. One was to grant complete sexual licence to both parties. "We love each other, we'll stay together forever, but sexual fidelity is a ridiculously outdated notion." To make it worse, they often added: "There is, however, one strict condition to be observed: we tell each other everything." On a lower social level wife-swapping was in vogue for a while, but this never really worked. As a rule, one party enjoyed his or her sexual freedom and the other party did not dare to confess that he or she hated every minute of it and suffered like hell lest he or she be regarded as a fossil. The "telling all" idea often became a device for torturing. The sadistic half of the marriage told all the details of his (usually, but not always, *his*) adventures, and the masochistic half had to suffer in silence and nod with a smile. All this could lead to nervous breakdowns, and sometimes suicides, but even these tragedies were attributed to other reasons because not to be "with it" – as the vogue phrase of that era had it – was worse than death. The arrangement, for a while, looked very progressive and broad-minded.

I am a trifle atavistic myself. I just would not like to think of my beloved girl jumping into bed with other chaps.

But what about my own traditional freedom, the idea that a fellow must have a bit of fun? Of course, it has suited me as it suits all men. But slowly I have been driven to the conclusion that this was not quite fair and what is sauce

64

for the goose is sauce for the gander. As a reasonably fair-minded gander I gritted my teeth, endured the frustrations, and remained faithful to my girl friend with a deep and nostalgic sigh for the lovely ideas which prevailed in the darkest Middle Ages.

The politicising of sex is the making of women. I fully and unequivocally accept the idea of equal rights for women. Not their literal equality – we have all heard the remark, *Vive la difference!* only too often – but their equal *rights*. I have known too many brilliant women and too many stupid men to have any doubt on this point.

On the other hand, I have also known a great many stupid women and a great many brilliant men. And this complicates matters more than somewhat.

In a country which has a female monarch and a female Prime Minister we seem to be, to say the least, on the right road. "Rubbish!" howls the militant feminist lobby. The Queen happens to be on the throne because she had no brothers – not even any much younger brothers. This is no feminist achievement. While Mrs Thatcher is an even worse case. She does not count, they say, because she is not a feminist. But she is a woman – indeed, she is an elegant, well-groomed and attractive woman. This response – the feminist chorus would reply – just shows up the male chauvinist pig in me. What does it matter whether a Prime Minister – or any woman – is attractive or ugly? Well, being a beautiful woman is no merit, but it will always be an advantage. But this is not the point. The point is this: to demand a militant feminist and not just a female in the country's leading position is female chauvinist piggery.

The Feminist Movement resembles the Trades Union movement in one important respect. The Trades Unions used to fight against real injustice, greed and exploitation, and every right-thinking man supported their struggle.

Then things started changing. While employers' greed and desire to exploit workers are not entirely matters of a distant past, the Unions have been gaining the upper hand. In spite of this, some go on fighting old and pointless battles, shouting the battle-cries of a bygone age. Most of them are unable to adjust to fast-changing conditions, rethink their positions and see their still very important role in new lights. Others go much further. The once-oppressed victims try to become the new oppressors and exploiters.

The extreme feminist sects are no better. When you suggest that things have improved, they call you a bloody reactionary and a fool. They will shout at you that a lot is still to be done as if these two statements – that much has been achieved but a lot remains to be done – were contradictory.

Many of them are lesbians and have a fanatical dislike of men. They would like to exclude men from society, from jobs, even from the family and do not even try to hide their hatred. "We have been oppressed long enough," they say, "it's high time to hit back." Fanaticism of this kind has condemned many revolutions to failure. If formerly oppressed classes or other groups, on gaining power, try to become the new oppressors (which they too often do) then the result, obviously, is not a reasonable and just society but a reversal of roles between oppressors and oppressed. This may seem fair at the moment of victory, but clearly it carries in itself the seeds of a new revolution – in this case a fight for "equal rights for men!" The desire to settle old accounts, to punish old oppressors (and men *have been* oppressors) is understandable; but understanding does not make it right. The oppression of the poor male by militant women is not a serious threat at the moment. But if the Lesbian Sisters had their way it would become reality tomorrow.

These groups are not trying to achieve justice, but to create a novel kind of injustice. I do not really care what they do in bed, that is their private affair. I grant them the right of total equality and also the right of privacy in their sex-life. But I do object when they try to dress up their perversity as a noble principle and higher ideology.

And what about those women who try to remain women in the old-fashioned sense of the word? They have to be educated and converted, is the reply. Converted, yes; but abused: no. It is not a base betrayal of their sex when they try to look pretty, wear jewellery and go on bearing babies. A woman has many rights. One among them is to remain a woman.

And what about those *men* who insist on their rights to remain women in the old-fashioned sense of the word? Some of them manage just that without provoking the wrath of the militant feminists, because there always existed an alliance between male and female homosexuals.

I personally could never see the sexual attraction of a fellow man, but tastes differ. A more liberal society has been eager to declare: what consenting adults do in private is their own business. The trouble is they don't think it so. The consenting adults have become a vociferous and assiduous minority. For a long time I watched them with great tolerance – after all, they had been the victims of violent persecution, repulsive hypocrisy, false moral indignation and downright stupidity. Society had regarded them as wicked and had demanded that either they should "reform themselves" and love the opposite sex – of which most of them were incapable – or give up sex altogether. If they refused, as they had to, they were ostracised in the best case, destroyed in the worst. The people hounding them were led, very often, by suppressed homosexuals. It was high time that society acknowledged: it is no shame to be a homosexual. But now the time has come to state clearly: "It is no particular glory either."

When I was a university student, every year a new Rector was elected. The Rector was the highest authority of the University, above the four Deans of the four faculties. One year it was the turn of the medical faculty, and the new Rector was a Professor of Venereal Diseases. He made an inaugural speech in which he informed us that the greatest men in history and art were all syphilitics. Syphilis, indeed, seemed to be a precondition of greatness. He mentioned many names. I remember only two – Julius Caesar and Napoleon – but on his roll of honour there were many giants. Perhaps quite a number on his list were not syphilitic at all, he simply claimed them because he admired them.

The Professor's views failed to gain world-wide recognition but I found this syphilocentric view of the world, this syphilocentric *Weltanschauung*, very original. The Prof

68

was so convincing that for a while I was eager to acquire syphilis by hook or by crook (it is usually by crook one acquires it). Luckily, I failed; but I *was* an ambitious young man.

Today the gays of our age have developed a gay-centric *Weltanschauung*. They proudly declare that all great artists, thinkers, writers, actors, dancers, fashion-designers and hairdressers – in other words: all who are responsible for true progress, from Plato through Wilde to Proust and Keynes – are or have been gay.

I do not object to this doctrine either. After all, it is innocent folly and as they leave Caligula, Charles II, Shakespeare, Picasso and Bertrand Russell to our camp, I do not complain. But they go on and on, and are becoming unsupportable bores. And to that I do object. Far from being "gay", they are – as a group, not as individuals – unbalanced neurotics. Like all former oppressed groups – Trades Unionists, women, etc – now they want to rule. I have absolutely no objection to being ruled by able homosexuals so long as they are selected because of their ability and not becuse of their homosexuality, but I do object to the idea that in order to count at all you have to prove – à la Nazis – that you have four homosexual grandparents.

Perhaps their excitement is just reaction to the first breath of fresh air. Very well, but we have reached the era of the second breath. They should calm down. Their problem is not the most important, let alone the only, problem of this world.

I accept that being homosexual is a genetic trait, like having blue eyes. But why do they make more noise than the blue-eyed people? Homosexuals, whether men or women, should stop fighting to rule our future. Their majority rule would exclude the very possibility of a future, so please, tolerate us poor, inartistic, squat, low and unoriginal heteros. It is just a little tolerance I am begging for. We can't help it either.

On Marriage

MARRIAGE IS quite a good institution but it does make a difference whom you marry.

The first and overwhelmingly important rule is that you must never marry a person with whom you are in love. The word *love* has a wide application. You may love your mother; you may love apple-pie; and you may love a television star whom you have never met in the flesh. Occasionally you may even love the person you marry and it is not always a bad thing – indeed, in certain cases it may help matters. But total independence, when you do not care a hoot for him or her, may be just as sound a basis for a lasting union. Mutual hatred – as we shall see – is not necessarily bad either. But, in any case, you must run away from him or her if you are *in love*. (This *he or she, him or her* business makes writing on certain subjects clumsy and tedious. So I shall stick to the rules of legal language: *he* implies *she* unless otherwise stated. There is no anti-feminist conspiracy in this method. I am not trying to subjugate the female sex and condemn it to eternal slavery, I am simply trying to be a shade more readable.)

Romantic novels are rubbish. Not only literary rubbish, which they are too, but their basic assumption that love is a sound foundation of future happiness is dangerous nonsense.

No one is less competent to choose a partner for life than a person in love. Being in love is an acute mental disease. It seems at the time to be less lethal than typhoid but occasionally it can be even more dangerous in its residual effects (a bad marriage, unwanted children etc). I am prepared to go so far as to say that being in love may be quite pleasant as long as it does not lead to a lasting union. I described the main symptoms of being in love, or infatuation, in an earlier work. They are as follows:

1. A charming young lady – or one not so charming and not so young – makes the silliest and most commonplace remark and you consider her wittier than Oscar Wilde, deeper than Pascal and more original than Bernard Shaw.

2. She calls you Pootsie, Bimby, Angelface or some other stupid and humiliating name, and you are enchanted and coo with delight.

3. She has no idea what the difference is between the EEC and the GLC, and you find this disarmingly innocent.

4. You expect her to behave like a cocotte towards you, and like a morbidly prim Victorian schoolgirl to everybody else. It may take you years to discover that the position is exactly the reverse.

5. Whenever she flirts with someone else and is rude to you, you buy her a huge bunch of flowers and apologise humbly. If she misbehaves seriously, you buy her jewellery.

You are expected to choose your future spouse when you are absolutely incapable of so doing, when you are in a condition to think silliness wisdom, affectation real charm, selfishness a good joke and an attractive face the highest of human achievements. You would never send a deaf man to buy your records, a blind man to buy your paintings or an illiterate to choose your books; but you expect to choose the person whom you are going to listen to more than to your favourite record, see more often than the pictures on your walls and whose remarks will be more familiar to you than the pages of your most treasured books – in a state of deafness, blindness and illiteracy. You may be fortunate: there are a great many good records, pictures and books around and even the deaf, blind and

71

illiterate may make a lucky dip. You may discover that there is nothing wrong in your choice, except that you bought a rousing march instead of a pastorale, a battle scene instead of a still life or a copy of *War and Peace* instead of *The Ideal Husband*.

Little wonder that Indian and other arranged marriages often prove more successful than love matches. A

choice made by parents is, as a rule, more objective and better considered than the impulse of an infatuated teenager. And even when parents make their choice for nothing wiser than financial considerations – even then, it may be a safer guide than being in love.

When I said that a great deal depends on whom you marry, I did not mean that you must wait for a so-called ideal. The first trouble with the "ideal" is that there is no such thing. Your ideal is not necessarily my ideal. You, a romantically inclined young lady, may dream of a fairy prince on a white horse. If you are unlucky you may get one. But another young lady may prefer a successful sales manager of a prosperous supermarket who is given the use of a 1400 cc company car. There is no such person as Mr Right. Or as Ms Right. Some brilliant men cannot bear stupid women, others cannot bear clever women. They spend all their working life with boringly intelligent females and, by the evening, they want to be refreshed by a little silliness and lack of profundity. How often have you heard the remark: "I am prepared to accept anything except a man without a sense of humour"? It is often made by singularly humourless women who could not in fact bear a man *with* a sense of humour. Sadists are generally believed to be quite unbearable partners but, of course, they are ideal for masochists. Even this is not universally true – nothing is universally true. Sometimes two sadists have a capital time together, tormenting each other all the time and enjoying every minute of it. Other sadists, on the other hand, are so cruel that they refuse to torment their masochist partner, thus making the masochist thoroughly unhappy.

One important point to remember in such sadist-masochist unions is this: the sadist is often caring, and indeed kind, as long as he can decide everything, as long as he can rule. Another point: the sadist needs the masochist as much as, or more than, the masochist needs him. (I am not speaking, of course, of thoroughgoing masochistic or sadistic perverts, just of masochistically or sadistically inclined people, i.e. of myself and of you, Gentle Reader, because all of us are either one of the other.) Not the most dangerous, but the most unattractive people in this category are the "hang-them, beat-them, flog-them, garrotte-them" brigade. They are preoccupied with violence without having the courage to commit it. Others should perform the flogging and hanging for their enjoyment.

The masochistic partner breaks down, cries, feels thoroughly unhappy and threatens to leave her sadistic partner. He tells her: the sooner you go the better. He is quite certain she would not dream of leaving and indeed she does not. That is: until one day, when she decides that enough is enough and packs her luggage. Then the sadist collapses. He needs her; his life is empty without her; he did not show his great and burning love but it is there and he will be a changed character. She relents and stays on. For three days things are better, but by the end of the week everything starts all over again and goes on as before. He does not change and cannot change. Both of them are really quite happy, even if they think themselves miserable. (*He* and *she* are interchangeable throughout this paragraph.)

Nowadays many people decide that they will not get married but will live together. That, usually, is a mistake. The right approach is this: we'll get married but will not live together.

Marrying is easy; living together is difficult. Many people cannot bear even their own company and would walk out on themselves if this were physically possible. Admittedly, young couples with babies cannot afford the luxury of two establishments (but people who want children should marry anyway). Young couples must occupy the same flat or house for the sake of the children. One-parent families often work miraculously well but a two-parent family is the easier solution, at least from the work-sharing point of view. There are, however, many people who do not want or cannot have children; divorced or widowed people who have had their children but now find new partners in life. When the new association starts they usually have two establishments. If they are wise they will keep them both. Then they can spend as much time together as they wish, but can retain privacy, solitude, days off – and this does not mean that they will love each other less. Indeed, they will love each other more. A beloved person who comes to have dinner with you almost every day is a joy; a woman or a man who is always under-foot and in your way is a nuisance. You may be tolerant and understanding – he must be *somewhere* (that's a law of nature) and, after all this is his home – but a nuisance remains a nuisance. And the whole point is: your home should *not* be his home.

The best marriage I have ever seen is between two doctor friends of mine. The man lives in Athens, the wife in Madrid. Two Mediterraneans, tuned to the same wavelength, two colleagues, yet people with different backgrounds. They meet three times a year and they are extremely happy together – when they *are* together. They are just as happy apart.

This is a good marriage. The arrangement, all the same, could be improved. If she stayed in Madrid but he lived in Tokyo and they met only once a year, that would be not just a good but the ideal marriage.

On the Power of the Weak

MOST PEOPLE WANT power, money and sex – that is the general belief. Many of them wonder anxiously: "How on earth can I attain power when I am so weak?" This is a silly question. It is like asking: "How can I live like a millionaire when I am poor?" Of course you can – and live better, without the worries of a millionaire. (For a detailed exposition of this thesis see my book *How to be Poor*.) It is the same with power for the weak, only more so. Indeed, the weaker you are, the more potentially powerful you are. The power of the mighty is provocative, challenging. It is a pleasure, sometimes a duty, to resist and defy it. But the power of the weak is truly terrifying.

Most of us who resist coercion, blackmail, and threats with admirable courage – succumb to the pleading of the weak. To help the weak, the poor, the miserable is an irresistible urge; it makes us feel noble and generous at a small cost. Or that's what we like to think. All the same, even the toughest, crudest and most unsensitive among us like to feel noble from time to time.

If a stentorian and authoritative voice makes an unreasonable demand on us – and adds, as it usually does: "And hurry up, don't dilly-dally!" – we are inclined to reply: "Go and do it yourself!" But if poor old Aunt Agatha asks us to drive seven miles to buy a piece of cheese-cake for her (it's available round the corner, too, but Auntie really likes only *that* cheese-cake), then who will be unkind enough to refuse? No, you will drive seven miles to get that wretched cheese-cake by lunch-time. Not for the sake of Aunt Agatha, of course. To hell with Aunt Agatha! For the sake of seeing yourself as a man who drives seven miles to get a piece of cheese-cake for his aged aunt (whom he heartily detests in the first place).

How many families are tyrannised by the weak, the old, the helpless, the disabled? How many hopeful lives are destroyed by them?

Once I mentioned to Arthur Koestler that I was supporting some cause – I forget now what it was – although I was far from being convinced that it really deserved my support. He replied: "One of the tragedies of life is that the victim is not always right." Alas, the victim may be awfully wrong and thoroughly loathsome. In principle, of course, you may condemn the injustice against him and yet reject him as an ally, but that is not so easy. You are either on one side or on the other. Similarly, some of the poor, the old, the sick, the miserable may be particularly unlovable, downright disgusting and cunning tyrants.

I am a good example of this, myself. All my life I have been cashing in on my mechanical imbecility. I cannot – and genuinely cannot – mend a fuse. Well, perhaps I genuinely cannot do it because I genuinely refuse to learn how to do it. And the same goes for many other skills. I used to have the same attitude about cooking – it is more comfortable if others cook for me – but I have overcome that particular aversion and by now I am not only a reasonably good cook, but quite an enthusiastic one. A lot of other dull jobs, as I have said, I still "cannot" do. So my dear friends and neighbours come in to help out the poor helpless old chap. They clean my car, sweep my patio, mend my electricity, sew on my buttons, etc. I am infinitely grateful and say so repeatedly. That boosts their ego; and saves me a lot of trouble and expense.

The truth is that the weak rule the world. They get away with everything. Here is another true story of how the weak can become – suddenly and unexpectedly – strong.

Before the Second World War I knew a man, Mr Bognár, who used to visit a friend and colleague of mine, another Hungarian journalist who was staying in the same boarding house as I. My friend was a clever chap, a real wizard, and Mr Bognár was desperate to know when war would break out. There were innumerable crises, many false alarms such as Munich, but Mr Bognár trusted my friend to tell him when the real thing would happen. He had to know this, he explained, because he wanted to buy red copper. "What do you need red copper for?" I asked naïvely. He did not need it and was not even quite sure what it was used for, but he knew one thing: at the beginning of World War One, his boss in Hungary had bought a large amount of red copper and he became a very rich man on it, because red copper was needed in wartime. Now Mr Bognár meant to emulate his former boss. "By the way," he added, addressing himself to my friend, "would you lend me a pound?" My friend, not a sentimental chap or a delicate diplomat, said that he most certainly would not. Not because he did not have a pound, he added, but because he did not trust Mr Bognár. He was, however, prepared to risk half a crown ($12\frac{1}{2}$p in decimal currency). Mr Bognár went on pressing, persuading and begging my friend to raise his offer but without success. He finally accepted half a crown. Mr Bognár kept on visiting us and in August 1939, after the Soviet-Nazi Pact, my friend told him that this was the real thing, war would break out very soon now. As we all know, it did. I heard later that Mr Bognár had bought his red copper, and I asked naïvely – with what money? The man who had seemed too untrustworthy to borrow £1 from my friend had, it now appeared, absolutely no difficulty in borrowing £50,000 from his bank. His red copper investment, by the way, worked perfectly. Mr Bognár became a rich man and died, many years later, as a millionaire in America.

A man who wishes to borrow one pound is a beggar; a

man who needs £50,000 is – obviously – a serious businessman. But the moral of this tale goes further. The weak man is kicked around and despised until he becomes *very* weak. A man who owes his bank £50 gets rude letters and threats. But if Mr Bognár had been unable to pay back the £50,000 he would have been in a commanding position. No small bank manager likes to report to head office that he had made a silly misjudgment, lent without security and lost a lot of money (and £50,000 was much more money in 1939 than it is today – although I would accept £50,000 even today from any bank). On a different level: Brazil and Mexico are, they say, almost bankrupt; at the same time they have only to whistle to get a few more billions from the World Bank and others because their bankruptcy would cause havoc and ruin on the international money-market and many large banks would fail all over the world. Their only strength is their weakness. Nobody cares about the United States. If the US makes a suggestion, other nations – particularly small nations – turn it down with special relish, just to show that they are not US colonies (which, of course, they often are). But whenever Brazil or Mexico utters a deep sigh, a few hundred million dollars arrive by telex.

Weakness rules the world. But it is not so easy to be weak. To achieve real, heart-rendering weakness requires a certain type of character, a certain amount of cunning and, in most cases, a great deal of bad luck. Fortune is a whimsical deity and she frowns only on the chosen few.

On Identity

"IDENTITY" IS ONE of the burning and tormenting non-problems of our age. I don't know who invented it as a new, burdensome problem; but I do know that writers, journalists and philosophes have picked it up with relish – there is a shortage of really good, new problems – and half of humanity now belives that "identity" is something important.

My son and his wife, who live in Lausanne in Switzerland, are planning to adopt a baby. The child will have to be an Indonesian baby. They went to Jakarta, saw the baby and, at the moment, are waiting for some bureaucratic decision. When serious and thoughtful people hear about their plan, they shake their heads anxiously and declare that this is a risky business. Of course it is, I quite agree. To adopt a baby is always a risky business – and there is some risk even in producing your own. But that's not what they have in mind, they reply: it will not be an easy thing for an Indonesian child and adolescent to live in Switzerland. There may be something in this, too, but – I tell them – he will not be living *only* in Switzerland. He will also live in his own family circle. Inside that family he will be fully accepted and loved. That is, if he is a nice little boy. If he turns out to be an unbearable brat, arrogant and destructive – which is extremely unlikely, judging by his adopting parents' views and characters – then I shall love him less, but that will have nothing to do with his not being a European. At the moment – and it is no good denying it – it is a Good

Thing being a European, since ours is the leading Continent in almost everything. The idea of European-ness is widely interpreted: Americans are Europeans, so are Australians and New Zealanders and so will be, in no time, the Japanese. Be that as it may, being a European is perhaps an advantage, but not a merit. In any case:

> It is purely accidental
> that you are an occidental . . .

At this stage of the discussion our serious friends interrupt me triumphantly: that is exactly what they mean: the child will have a grave problem of identity.

Wrong again. He may indeed have problems. He may be rejected and mocked by some young fools in school whose only claim to superiority is the colour of their skin. Young fools become old fools in no time and the problem will not disappear too quickly. But the problem that little François is going to meet is a problem of stupidity and prejudice, not a problem of identity.

He will be a child, born in Indonesia, adopted by a Swiss couple, brought up and educated in Lausanne – and that's that.

This serious and bewildering non-problem has been pursuing me almost all my life. Only yesterday (the day before writing this, I mean) I gave an interview to a foreign newspaper and was pressed hard about my "identity". Am I more Hungarian than English? I said I did not care, did not know and had no idea how to measure it. This was not accepted for an answer. I tried to convey that I was both and neither: I was myself.

I am sure quite a few people strongly disagree with me. I am trying to sweep a problem under the carpet, they will say. Most people, they will maintain, want to know who and what they are.

No doubt about that. Most people prefer to know about their family background. Many people dislike their family but are extremely proud of it at one and the same time. Many others find it disturbing not to have sufficient information about their origins. But what does this really mean? Your family background will not define you; the length of the list of your ancestors will not make you a better man. After all, we all have exactly the same number of ancestors even if some of us cannot recall anyone beyond our grandparents. Ultimately you are what you are and it is utterly irrelevant whether your family tree goes back fifty or five hundred years.

There is another peculiar contradiction in this desperate search for identity. You have found your identity (this is the general belief) as soon as you have found your individuality. Once you have established that you are not just a member of a herd, a horde, a bevy or a flock but an individual, you are supposed to have found your identity. But amazingly, the next step is: you must find out to which nation, family, tribe, horde, flock or bevy you belong, otherwise you have no *real* identity.

I am convinced that the real *unit* of humanity is man. (And *man* also means woman.)

Identity is a cloak, a mere mask, a cover. Below that "identity" is a person, a unique human being, and that is you. And me. Don't try to hide behind your cloak or mask: face yourself naked. Your belly will be a trifle larger than it looks in a well-cut suit; your breasts – if you happen to be a lady – may be a little larger or smaller than you would like

On V.I.P.s

I HAVE ALWAYS been astounded by the expression V.I.P. – Very Important Person – because it implies that there are V.U.P.s – Very Unimportant Persons – too. Indeed, it implies that the bottom 99 per cent of humanity are V.U.P.s.

Occasionally, I find myself in the V.I.P. lounge at an airport. (The airlines are really responsible for this V.I.P.

snobbery.) I am surrounded by self-important business-men with bulging brief-cases. There is a telephone in front of each of us, the idea being that we V.I.P.s cannot lose even one precious moment without giving instructions to our countless minions. As they are all talking busily, I feel that I must use the telephone, too. I have absolutely nothing to say to anyone, so I wake up my girl-friend here, a male chum there. I explain my position and a sleepy voice tells me to go to hell. I quite see their point, but put down the receiver with the face of a Very Important Person who has just settled yet another terribly important matter – need I say? – triumphantly.

People peer into the V.I.P. lounge with admiring eyes, or scrutinise us when we walk out to board our plane. I feel inclined to address a little speech to them: "Please, don't be taken in by this charade. It is very rarely that I am invited to this lounge. I assure you I am not any more important than any of you. But I hasten to add: neither am I any less important, whoever you may happen to be."

Very Important Person. Important to whom? A general is supposed to be more important than a private and, indeed, more important than a brigadier; the President of a company is more important than a lowly clerk or a mere Vice-President; a rich man is supposed to be more import-ant than a poor one and a monarch than his subjects.

Every man is not only a unit (see previous chapter) but a complete universe in himself. Nothing and nobody is more important than he (or she – see previous chapter once again). In some cases of extreme elation and enthusiasm you may be ready to sacrifice your life for a cause or a person, but such moments are rare and, in any case, the decision should be yours. You may regard – perhaps just in the heat of the moment – the cause as being more important than your life.

In normal circumstances, however, if you suffer from a bad toothache, that becomes the most important thing in the world. Unilateral Nuclear Disarmament may be a decisively important issue for you but it will dwindle into insignificance compared with your agonising toothache. Every hungry beggar will regard a good meal as more important than the civil wars in Central America. Every man who has just lost his job, will find securing a weekly £80 for himself much more important than a £430 million rebate due to Britain from the EEC.

Everyone, in the final analysis, is the one and only V.I.P. in his own eyes. Philosophers have posed the problem: does the outside world really exist beyond our perception? Or is it only an illusion? Is that book really in our drawer after we close the drawer or does it suddenly reappear when we open it again? Philosphers can be extremely foolish. I personally suspect that the world does exist and find that the book is never in the drawer. Not finding books in places where I think I put them is normal in my case – not para-normal at all.

But if those philosphers are right and the world does really exist only in our own personal perception, then we are not only the only V.I.P.s in the world. We are the only Ps.

Rank, position and wealth have nothing to do with your importance. Neither do figures and statistics. I have never heard of a Chinese mother who lost a child, remarking: "Well, what does it matter? There are another thousand million Chinese and the loss of one Chinese means really nothing."

When a terrible epidemic is abating, the newspapers may report triumphantly: "Only one dead!" A great improvement, particularly if on the previous day 124 people died. Glorious news for everything – except for the one man who died. He will not rub his hands with glee and say: "Wonderful news! Only I died." He will selfishly disregard all statistics and know – if he does know – that he is a hundred per cent dead.

No, don't be modest. You are a closed-in world to yourself and no one – *no one!* – is more important than you are. This truth, however, implies a regrettable other truth, which is quite unbearable for a lot of people and poisons many lives: no one is less important, either.

On Putting Your Foot in It

I THINK IT WAS President Eisenhower who remarked about his Secretary of State, John Foster Dulles: "Whenever he opens his mouth, he puts his foot in it."

We all keep putting our foot in it even if not with the regularity of an American Secretary of State.

It is no good trying to extricate your foot. If you say of a poem in a magazine that you have "Never seen such trash," and it turns out that the man to whom you make the remark is the poet himself, you may feel embarrassed. But that's about all you can do. You may stutter something about different people having different tastes, perhaps – but it is no good declaring with conviction that when you said "trash" you really meant that the poem was a near-masterpiece.

The more desperately you try to extricate your foot, the deeper it will sink into the morass.

This happened long ago but I still shudder when recalling it. I went to a party with my wife. I never recognise anybody but she is very good at it, so it was her duty – which she had always performed magnificently – to advise me who this or that person was. Either she had a chance of whispering the name into my ear before the person arrived; or else she greeted the person loudly by his or her name, but she always conveyed the necessary information somehow. On this occasion she failed miserably. A girl – the lover of a close friend of ours – joined us . It was a rare occasion: I recognised her without a moment's hesistation but my wife made the odd remark: "It's almost uncanny . . . You resemble Jenny X to such an extent . . . "

The lady interrupted my wife coolly: "I *am* Jenny X."

This was pretty awful. She was not a casual acquaintance but a close friend. We saw them regularly and my wife had met her twenty times, at least. Feeling guilty, she asked chattily: "How is David?"

Upon which Jenny burst out crying. When – after a minute or two – she was able to speak, she asked: "Didn't you hear?"

She did not need to tell us *what*. They had obviously split up. My wife, still determined to make up for her blunders, now told her: "You see, Jenny, every coin has two sides. You always wanted David to marry you and he refused. How much better it is now that you never married."

She replied through her tears: "We got married two months ago."

At this point my wife really ought to have thrown in her hand. One should know when one is beaten and retreat with as much dignity as one can muster. But she was a true heroine and held the fort. She said: "Well, such sad things do happen. Still, better that it should happen now than when you are forty or so."

Jenny was sobbing again: "I am forty-five."

At this moment my wife did not only give up but she became visibly furious. Before she could cry out: "In that case go to bloody hell!" I dragged her away.

It was after this incident that I formulated the law: *if you put your foot in it, leave it in.*

How Many Sides to the Coin?

IN THE PREVIOUS chapter I quoted my wife saying that every coin has two sides. That is another popular fallacy, reflecting an "either-or", "yes or no" attitude. Most coins have more than two sides – ten or a dozen in complicated cases.

One small example.

Unemployment is a Bad Thing. This, undoubtedly, is true. It is bad for the unemployed, bad for the State, bad for general morale. So the simple solution would be to fight unemployment and abolish it. This still remains as a remote, theoretical aim but the third side of the coin is to turn unemployment into a Good Thing. Many unemployed find a secret source of income and fail to declare it, which makes unemployment quite desirable, at least for a few people who make an effort to lose their jobs. A fourth side of the coin affects the state: increasing unemployment (voluntary or enforced) means more money paid out in benefits and much less money – thousands of millions less – gathered in taxes. A fifth side of the coin is trying to solve this problem by employing extra tax-men. (The latest news is that a special tax squad has been increased from 70 to 850.) This step decreases the number of unemployed at least among taxmen, some of whom will thus cease to be active on the black economy (driving minicabs, selling the products of their gardens, etc).

The sixth side of the coin is this: what to do with those who are caught in tax evasion? They should stand trial, the "two-siders-of-the-coin" would claim. But the authorities would not dream of it. Some of the schemes – which would become public at the trials – are so ingenious that they'd better remain secrets.

So here is a simple little coin with six sides. In some cases – in the cases of burning injustice, for instance, or of patently aggressive war – decent men can only take one possible view. These are the rare coins with one side only. Yes, some coins may have *one* side; but I have never seen a coin with two.

On Not Feeling Guilty

A PSYCHOLOGIST friend of mine once asked me to collaborate with him on a book. I was quite ready to do so. He explained that in order to know what we were talking about I ought to go through psychoanalysis. I refused. He said that I must do it, for two months. I replied that I felt no need for being psychoanalysed – besides two months was not enough to achieve anything. But he insisted and I gave in.

In the end, the book came to nothing but for two months I lay on the couch twice a week. One of the first subjects to be discussed was guilt. Did I feel terribly guilty? No, not at all.

This surprised him. This is not the type of answer a psychoanalyst wishes to hear. If you are lying on an analyst's coach, you should bloody well be a tormented soul, devoured by guilt.

"You must be a man of impeccable virtue," he told me saracastically. "Always doing the right thing. Immaculate character. Much better than most of us."

"Quite the contrary, I am afraid," I replied. "Not immaculate at all. More maculate, in fact, than most. I commit all the mistakes and crimes most of us commit, but I – unlike more decent people – don't ever feel guilt-ridden and suicidal after my misdeeds."

My friend was outraged. He thought I was making fun of people's guilt-feelings and was not taking their problems seriously. Guilt-feeling – he explained with a lot of personal heat – was the most destructive of all human torments.

Perhaps. I was not taking it lightly. I was also aware that it is as effective and sensible to tell a guilt-ridden man: "Don't feel guilty" as it is to tell a man with bronchitis not to cough. All the same, all I can do is to state my own attitude to the problem.

There are two types of guilt which may torment you. Let's suppose you fraudulently ruined your business partner, or ran away with your best friend's wife. In such cases you might feel guilty because you *are* guilty. The other type is a neurotic guilt-feeling. You feel responsible for imaginary crimes, you carry burdens which have nothing to do with you. You blame yourself for the mistakes of others, you feel responsible for the rotten state of the world. Psychiatrists may help you – or more precisely: may help you to help yourself. The one way out – with their help or without it – is to turn your feeling of guilt into a constructive drive instead of letting it grow and destroy you.

This is extremely difficult to achieve. It requires deep self-knowledge, above-the-average intelligence and, above all, strong creative impulses. Arthur Koestler wrote in *The Invisible Writing:* "I believe, that if properly canalised, the consciousness of guilt may become a powerful and constructive driving force; and that the anguish which accompanies it should be regarded as income tax paid in emotional currency."

Your mistakes and crimes may be divided, once again, into two types. There are those which cannot and those which can be rectified. I do not suggest that even if something cannot be rectified you should just shrug your shoulders. Learn the lesson by all means: try not to commit the same mistake again. But do not let it eat you up. You must accept yourself as you are. It would be so nice if you were a knight in shining armour . . . but I bet you are not.

You are in a worse position if you know you have followed the right path, yet you have caused hardship to

others. You may, for example, have pursued a just claim for damages to which you are fully entitled in law and in morality, and someone may be ruined as a result. You may have regained a house to which you have every right, and the person who had to get out may be homeless. You may have taken some perfectly legitimate action against a crook, and as a result his marriage may be ruined – or perhaps he may even have committed suicide. If, in such a case, there is a chance that you can get your rights without causing any such tragic results, then seize that chance; or if you are a truly sensitive soul, let your rights go (but do not suppose, in that case, that the crook will feel guilty in his turn and will pay up. Not bloody likely!) In cases such as these you must weigh up all the pros and cons before you act, in the full awareness that your gain – your perfectly rightful gain – may be someone else's loss. If you decide to go ahead, then do not moan because something that is good for you turns out to be ruinous for someone else. Particularly if he happened to ask for it.

My ideal in this respect is President Truman. He had to make the most harrowing decision any human being ever had to make: should the atom-bomb be dropped on Hiroshima, or not. He consulted his advisers, weighed up the argument, did not dither. He made a decision. The bomb must be dropped. Having made the decision, he went to bed and enjoyed a good night's sleep.

I flatter myself that if I had found myself President of the United States in 1945, I would have made exactly the same decision. Truman also said: "If you are afraid of the heat, keep out of the kitchen." Nobody is forced to become President, or even Vice-President, of the United States. You choose to go into that kitchen by your free will, and once you are in the kitchen, the heat may become terrific. You either order that bomb to be dropped or not. But you cannot drop it and avoid casualties. War is war and if you are responsible for hundreds of thousands – indeed, millions – of lives, you must face your responsibilities. Dropping the bomb may be a dreadful act; but deciding not to drop it may have consequences no less dreadful. I would have made the same decision as Truman, knowing that my decision – horrible though it was – would save hundreds of thousands of American lives. Japan entered the war as an aggressor, and to save Japanese lives was not the primary consideration of the President of the United States. Yet, even on that count I would not hesitate, knowing that the bomb, however horrible its consequences, demanded fewer Japanese victims than battles from island to island would have demanded, and that the war would be over in two days instead of two years. Knowing that I would save American as well as Japanese lives, and shorten the war, I would have ordered the dropping of the bomb; and having made the decision, I would have gone to bed and would have slept just as soundly as President Truman did. And would never have felt guilty about my decision ever after.

Ageism

OF ALL THE *isms* bedevilling our era – racism, anti-semitism, sexism, feminism, etc – ageing, the mutual hatred of the young and the old, is the most ludicrous. This antagonism is much older than feminism or racism. In the old days women accepted their inferior position and different races had few contacts. But people were always born fairly young and grew old slowly (some feel not slowly enough), and the old always hated the young and *vice versa*. This hatred is as old as the human race and much older than civilisation. The text of the first hieroglyphics solved was the lament of old men about the new generation which just did not have the sterling virtues of the old (i.e. the writer himself). Degeneration of humanity was inevitable in the near future. That was some five thousand years ago. We have been degenerating ever since. Human progress may be just the story of our degeneration.

I call ageism more stupid than other isms because a black man never becomes white, a white man never becomes black, a man never (or hardly ever) becomes a woman, but a young man always becomes old, except when he does not. Indeed, this is the first truth to be remembered: *every old man has been young; but not every young man will grow old*.

There is no great virtue in having been born in a particular year – whether it is a recent or an ancient date. Many people find their childhood and adolescence intolerable. I am not one of them. But if I were given the rare chance of living my life again I would decline with thanks. Once it was beautiful; but once was enough.

To revere old men – as many societies do – for their age alone, is just as silly as the more modern habit of revering the young. Help the old, by all means. To offer your seat in the tube to a nonagenarian is nicer than to watch with amusement how his legs tremble. On the other hand, not every old man is decrepit and not every young man is vigorous, talented and suitable for every job. Youth, machismo and inexperience do not qualify you to do everything.

Some years ago we had the London Hard Court Championships at Hurlingham Club. The loudspeaker called two men to play singles. A young specimen of true machismo, a sunburnt idol, surrounded by four admiring females, slowly rose and then caught sight of his adversary, an old friend of mine. This opponent was a white-haired gentleman, practically bent in two because he had (I knew this but, of course, it was not visible) two artificial hips. The sunburnt athlete threw a contemptuous glance at his opponent and was quite annoyed. What a waste of time. He turned to his woman friends and said: "I'll be back in a few minutes."

He was. Soundly beaten.

Old men *may* have a great deal of energy; young men cannot possibly have a lot of experience. Not every boy of eighteen would make an outstanding general or prime minister. Admittedly, neither does every general or prime minister (in his or her forties or fifties) make an outstanding general or prime minister. Nor is everyone in his seventies necessarily a brilliant President or First Secretary of a Party.

The young are terrified of looking at the old: "That's me, forty years on." But there is only one way of avoiding old age: to die young. Just as many Jews are anti-semitic, so many old people are ageists. They hate old people because they hate themselves. This hatred is often fully justified: they *are* hateful. I happen to accept myself as an aged youth. I love the young, wish them well, forgive them that they are often silly, conceited and boring. Youth is one deficiency that certainly will be cured in time. Which does not mean that silly, conceited and boring young men do not grow into silly, conceited and boring old men.

There is a Chinese proverb (a real one, not one invented by me) which says: "Look forward, not back." This applies to people at any age. If you are seventy, plan for seventy-three and do not moan over the bygone days when you were twelve or sixty-seven.

The adoration of the young is ludicrous from another point of view, too. It is silly to cherish and glorify the one characteristic that is bound to disappear. And disappear fast.

The future does belong to the young and so it should be. Attlee's old quip has an eternal validity. When he was asked, on his eightieth birthday: "How do you like being old, Lord Attlee?" he replied: "When I think of the alternative I like it very much." I personally do not mind – as long as I remain healthy and active – getting old. In fact, I would not mind getting older still.

Many people try to stop the march of time. It is not easy. Foolish octogenarians believe that lovely young girls fall in love with them because they are so lovable, so irresistible and, in any case – "age does not matter". The girls do marry them; not because they are loving wives but because they are aspiring widows.

Anyway, it is a contemptible habit of old fogeys to want younger and younger women and to turn away from their partners of a lifetime because they, too, grow old.

A very old man in bed with a very young woman is obscene; but a shared life, with a common past and common memories, common sufferings, joys, love, quarrels, defeats and triumphs is something beautiful.

When a young man wishes to make love, he is a virile fellow; when an old man does the same, he is a dirty old

man. The only difference between a virile athlete and a dirty old man is a few years. We all know about the desires and activities of old men. But what about old women? When a 85-year-old duchess (I forget her name) was asked in the Court of Louis XIV: "At what age does a woman cease to be interested in sex?" she replied: "If you want to know that, you must ask an older woman than I."

Is there a secret of eternal youth?

In an old men's home, among the aged and decrepit, there is one little old man who seems to have more energy and vivacity than the rest. He moves a little faster, he has a better appetite and even jumps up to open the door for others.

"What is your secret?" someone asks him. "What sort of life did you lead? Did you stick to a strict diet?"

He laughs.

"I always ate like a horse. Three big meals a day, fat, cholesterol, sugar – the lot."

"Hm. Have you been a teetotaller?"

"I drank a bottle of brandy every day. And wine with my meals. And a few drinks in between."

"And what about women?"

"At least one woman a day. Often two. Sometimes three."

"Good God," says another old man admiringly. "That's really amazing. And how old are you?"

"Twenty-seven."

No, we have not found the secret of eternal youth. But the secret of eternal old age has been solved.

How to Die

1. As an Individual

IT IS A GOOD THING that we all die. We should rejoice in this instead of bemoaning the fact.

Imagine a world in which all the human beings ever born are still around. Imagine how difficult it would be for a Sumerian hunter to understand – let alone enjoy – *Dallas* or *Coronation Street*. Or for a Hittite shepherd to learn to use the knife and then to accept the rule that he must not put it into his mouth. Napoleon himself would find it difficult to understand President Reagan's Middle Eastern or Central American strategy (not that I find it easy). There would be insuperable difficulties about dress, food, manners, and language. Poor Pericles would not understand a single word Andreas Papandreou might say to him in modern Greek. But all the problems of gastronomy, etiquette, customs and understanding would dwindle to nothingness when we came to sheer numbers. In the case of general immortality (or resurrection, with which we are also threatened) even the ablest Minister of Pensions would find his job embarrassing. It is not so easy today, either, but if the working population were 0.000000017 per cent of the total (and half of that working population were still out of work), the Minister would start longing for a little mortality – probably his own in the first place. Imagine the crowds in the supermarket. The shortage of sausages, the queues at the check-outs. Imagine the "geriatric rush-hours" in London, where after 9.30 in the morning old age pensioners can travel free on public transport at the flash of a card: the buses would be crammed with Romans and Vikings who had been doddering about with their spears and horned helmets for a thousand years or more. And if people survived, why not animals? Enough of anthropic jingoism! But just think of the mess in the streets that *all* the dogs who had ever lived would make.

Even if we dismiss the problems of humanity in general and of ministers of pensions in particular, the plight of the individual would be awful, too. It is all very well to dream of everlasting life, but after the first two hundred and twenty-five years it would become pretty boring. No end to those weaknesses in chest and bladder, those troublesome toe-nails . . . and apart from those afflictions, surely the whole thing would become monotonous and tiresome.

Home sapiens, as we call ourselves (though of course no bear or rattlesnake of average intelligence would give us that name), is the only animal that knows it is going to die.

And he cannot face this knowledge. All our philosophies –
the whole lot – are based on preoccupation with death. We
try to avoid the unavoidable, refuse to accept the evidence
which we see around us every day. Of course, there is such
a thing as very tragic death: the death of someone young, a
death that is violent or painful, and the *waste* of any life –
all these are terrible. But even the death of a young person
is often more harrowing for the survivors than for the one
who dies – and anyway, I am not concerned here with
such heart-rending tragedies. I am concerned with the
abject and contemptible fear of the fact that life ends in
death which can make the whole of life miserable for some
people.

A man who lets his fear of death overshadow most of his
life is a neurotic fool. A man who, after the age of about
sixty-five, does not think of the fact that he will not live for
ever is another type of fool: an insensitive or a cowardly
one.

Luckily, I can answer some of the most tormenting
questions of philosophy. 1. *What is the aim of life?* The
answer is: *nothing*. 2. *What happens to us after death?* The
answer again: *nothing*.

Let me explain. Life has no *universal* aim. We are not
here to celebrate the Glory of God. We have not been
created *ad majorem Dei gloriam*. God cannot be quite so
modest as to find the performance of humanity the proof of
final glory and majesty.

But if life has no *universal* aim, it does have, it should
have, a specific aim. The aim of *your* life is what you make
it to be. There is no life – not even the most unfortunate
and miserable person's life – which is void of pleasure,
beauty and love, as long as he is ready to make the best of
what he has and as long as he is not eaten up by envy and
jealousy.

You may find that the aim of your life is to devote it to
your children; or to birds; or to the enjoyment of Nature.
You may live in order to express yourself in one way or

another; to listen to good music and see beautiful pictures (or to listen to bad music and see lousy pictures); to read books on mathematics or to watch Match of the Day; to keep fit; to learn Spanish, Urdu or Albanian . . . The list is endless. It is utterly unimportant whether you achieve your goal or not as long as the pursuit fills your life and gives you satisfaction. Forget about money, fame and success as the so-called aims of life. Rich people are not *ipso facto* happier than others. And Shakespeare cares precious little whether *Hamlet* when performed today is a success or not.

I claim to have been a happy man. Not that all my life has been a giggle. When someone kicked me it hurt me as it hurts others. But I have used my limited ability skilfully, enjoyed what I was doing and even made a modest living out of it. I do not care a damn whether my own *Hamlet* will be read in a hundred or in ten years' time. Koestler remarked once that he would swap ten readers today for one in ten years' time and a hundred readers today for one in a hundred years' time. I would not. Read *How to be a Guru* today and let posterity look after itself. I wish the twenty-first century better Mikeses than I was able to provide for my own century.

It is *this* side of the grave you must make your life. Naturally it is more difficult for some than for others; but everyone, without exception, can find a great deal of beauty in his own life.

There is one inherent problem in my attitude. Those who believe in an after-life cannot be disappointed – if there is none, they will never find out their mistake. But if I am wrong, I shall learn how wicked I have been and it will be most embarrassing to find myself in purgatory. But I accept the risk.

I am – like all of us – a guest on this planet. Let's make the most of our brief appearance. Let's take second helpings when offered. But when the party is over, we should take our hats, bow and depart in peace. "Thank you for the party, I won't come again."

We shall all find being dead far from unpleasant. Not exactly fun, but far from unpleasant. *Dying* may be unpleasant, although with luck it can be quick and painless. But being dead is easy; child's play, in fact. Death is non-existence. We are used to it. We did not exist two hundred, two thousand, or two million years ago, so why should we be bothered by non-existence in the twenty-second or the forty-sixth century?

To accept the idea of death does not mean that you should mourn your demise throughout a lifetime. *Live as if you would live forever.* A few days ago my friends and I celebrated the eighty-fifth birthday of a very fine, lovable and happy man. He is in excellent shape and in perfect mental condition. There were fourteen of us around the table: two other octogenarians, about half a dozen over seventy and two babes, in their late fifties. Our guest of honour, replying to the toast, finished his speech by saying: "And when any of you, gentlemen, reach the age of eighty-five . . . " for a moment he sounded sombre and thoughtful, but he changed his tone: " . . . then just let me know and we shall celebrate together."

That's the spirit.

2. As a Species

It has often been explained that Hiroshima changed the fate of humanity. Before the first atomic bomb exploded – we are told – human beings were aware of individual death, but since Hiroshima we must get used to the idea of the death of the species. And that is supposed to be unbearable.

It is not unbearable at all; besides, there is nothing new in the threat.

There are a few people about who cannot bear the idea that after their demise life will go on, flowers will bloom in the spring tra-la, and children will laugh. They would feel much more comfortable if the whole world died with them. Luckily, these people are not too numerous. Most of us, indeed, are glad to know that after our death our children and grandchildren will go on living and we wish them happier lives than ours, however happy ours may have been.

Few people care much about the fate of the species beyond their great-great-grandchildren, and humanity's survival after AD 2320 – whatever we may dutifully mumble – is not a matter of harrowing concern for most of us.

Anyway, the fact – and it is a fact – that the species will not last for ever is something that we had better accept. Humanity is just as mortal as the individual human being.

Humanity is about a million years old – a newcomer on the earth, a mere babe in cosmic terms. If we are lucky, we may last another million years, but that's all. And we will last that long only if there are no nuclear or other accidents or cosmic disasters. This seems to be good enough for most people. If we do not genuinely worry beyond the age of our great-great-grandchildren, then few of us can become hysterical at the prospect of our species dying a million years from now. But a million years – from the point of view of the universe – is a fleeting moment, and to speak of the immortality of the human race is nonsense.

There are, we are told, another million inhabited planets in our own galaxy alone; and few of their inhabitants would blink an eyelid if they learnt, somehow, that one species on one of these planets had died out or committed suicide.

You must also bear in mind that a nuclear disaster would not extinguish humanity, only a major part of it.

I am not speaking of the survivors in shelters – rich people, members of the cabinet, the leader of the opposition and high-ranking civil servants. Once I asked an eminent nuclear physicist whether people in those shelters had a chance of survival. Yes, he said: unless the shelters suffered a direct hit, which is improbable, they have a very good chance of surviving. But there will remain the problem of radiation and they must be extremely careful not to emerge from their shelters for two-hundred-and-twenty years or say two-hundred-and-fifty, to be on the safe side.

No, I am not building shelters. I am neither rich enough, nor am I the leader of the opposition. Nor would I go down into one if I were invited. If London blows up, I claim the honour of blowing up with it. Perhaps I would think differently if I were twenty-one – and I wish the best of luck to all those, young or old, who do think differently.

So it is not the survivors in the shelters that I have in mind. No nuclear attack, or series of attacks, will destroy *all* humanity. People in the depths of Africa or in the jungles of South America will survive. All they will need is several hundred years to reach a sufficient degree of education and technical knowledge to start it all over again. They will find a computer here, an electric shaver or a TV set there – all will help. They will re-establish what we call – and they, no doubt will also call – civilisation.

And even if *all* human beings are wiped out, there are

other animals on this planet who will surely survive. It was Anatole France who foresaw the giant ant – an extremely intelligent and social animal – as the successor of mankind, the ruling species on earth. The ant needs only a little time: a few hundred thousand years, no more.

If humanity blows itself up with nuclear weapons, it will be a clear case of suicide. And what's wrong with suicide? One of the silliest and most hypocritical of all *dicta* is that suicides are cowards. They are specially brave people. Suicide needs great courage – greater than survival. And whose life is it, anyway?

To speak of the sanctity of human life is, in almost all cases, equally hypocritical. We sermonise about the sanctity of human life but approve of wars in good causes: causes, in other words, which we approve of – and we invariably approved either one side or the other. And what about the sanctity of animal life? Why is a man more sacred than a cow – especially as we talk so much about sacred cows? If we do really believe in the sanctity of life, we must say good-bye to beef, to grouse and to the glorious twelfth of August.

I personally stick to my principle, expressed in a previous chapter. We kill our cattle and our poultry because we want to eat them. We do not kill them because it is right to kill them, because it is justified, because we are entitled to do so. We kill them because we like fillet steak. This is not a noble reason – not worthy of any philosopher or theologian – but, at least, it is true.

Many of those who firmly believe in the sanctity of life, go on contemplating the nuclear massacre of humanity with apparent equanimity. We ordinary citizens can do very little about it. Unilateral nuclear disarmament would create more dangers, instead of alleviating them.

Suicide, however – as I have said – is not cowardice. People who commit suicide, are our unfortunate but brave – sometimes disturbed – brethren. They deserve our respect, not our derision. A sick man who cannot bear any more physical pain or the thought of becoming a vegetable, decides to throw away his one and only life. We should stand by his grave, hat in hand, with head bowed and with tears in our eyes.

The same goes for humanity. There are clear signs that humanity, too, is sick and intent on suicide. We should be ready to respect that decision, too . . . but our position is undoubtedly somewhat complicated. We are involved in humanity's death, but not involved in the decision making. The sad and premature death of our species – which may originally have been destined for a better fate – will be the suicide of something mortally sick, and our proper reaction would be to stand by its grave, hat in hand, with head bowed and with tears in our eyes. But how to do it when we shall have neither hats nor heads?

Envoi

THAT, THEN, IS my message. Readers who have followed me right through must have gathered the impression that I am of a happy-go-lucky disposition. But I am no cynic, and do believe in quite a few things: for example, in the power of books, particularly books written in London by ex-refugees. I have in mind, primarily, my colleagues Karl Marx and Sigmund Freud, whose works (although more boring than mine) made quite an impression on the world. (Admittedly, Freud wrote many of his before he arrived in London – but I am open-minded enough to grant that being an ex-refugee in London is not

the *only* condition for writing an influential book. Natives such as Charles Darwin have sometimes done quite well, and so have a few outright foreigners, such as Copernicus with his *On the Revolution of Heavenly Spheres* and Galileo with *Siderius Nuncius*.)

All the above writers changed the fate of humanity. The author of the present volume (that's me) is quite prepared to make a lesser impact. But here it is: a message of hope, of optimism, of making the most of life. Here it is: a thesis that proclaims happiness, or at least contentment, to be within the reach of everyone. Once you have grabbed a little contentment, satisfaction, good humour and optimism, do not be ashamed of it, as most intellectuals seem to be, and do not throw it out of the window. But whether you do or not is up to you. I have given my recipe.

I must admit that I have offered no solution. Nobody ever has. There *are* no solutions.

Every problems solved creates new and unforeseen problems (see the chapter on 'How Many Sides to the Coin?'). The creation of Trades Unions remedied long-standing injustices and liberated workers from shocking conditions, but even Tony Benn himself would not deny that the increasing power of the Unions has created grave problems in society. In Third World countries independence has only too evidently created more problems than it solved. Or take the abolition of slavery: it caused social and economic shocks which reverberate through certain societies until this day. This, of course, does not mean that we should say 'Let's abolish Trade Unions, re-occupy the empire and re-establish slavery'. But it does mean that even the most necessary solution of a problem will *always* create other problems (some of them, with luck, minor ones) which have to be solved in their turn and the solution of which will create new problems again. And so on, endlessly.

Which is just as well. Without problems humanity would die of boredom, which wouldn't be much better than committing nuclear suicide.

I should like to say good-bye with a modern parable. It's moral is that all you need in life is good spirits, determination and a little luck. The hero of this story is my ideal, and he should also be the ideal of everyone who has benefitted – however little – from these pages.

He is a French friend of mine called Henri D: the only member of his extremely wealthy and well-known family who, during the German occupation of France, behaved like a decent French patriot. When a vast fortune was restored to the guilty members of his family – collaborationists to a man – he not unnaturally expressed dissatisfaction. The family united against him, cheated him of his share and kicked him out of the family business. While they sat there enjoying their riches, Henri was left penniless and plagued by petty worries.

Henri did not despair. He was almost in rags when I first met him, but in excellent fighting spirits, full of enthusiasm for life, and completely without bitterness. He had just formed a small publishing firm and was absolutely determined to succeed and prosper.

I did not meet him again for about fifteen years, by which time he was a rich man. This is the story he told me.

"You know those success stories about American millionaires, like the one about the banker who was ruined in the great crash so he bought himself a pound of apples and sold it at a few cents profit, and then bought two pounds and made a few more cents. And so on and so on until today he's the greatest fruit importer-exporter in the whole of the United States? Well, my story is vaguely similar. You remember I founded that little publishing firm? I worked hard, was very cautious, lived very modestly and eighteen months later went bankrupt. I did not lose heart and give up. I started again, and this time I worked even harder, was even more circumspect and lived even more frugally, so this time it took me two full years to go bankrupt. Then I inherited one hundred and eighty million francs from my grandmother, and I have never had another worry."

You remember that I told you earlier in this book to be careful in your choice of parents? You should be equally careful when you choose your granny.